Coaching Psychology: Integrating Mental Health & Life Coaching

Published by Youth Success Coaching, LLC.

Fort Myers, Florida, USA

Copyright © 2024 by Sheryl Ellis. All rights reserved.

No part of this publication may be reproduced, distributed, or transmitted in any form or by any means, including photocopying, recording, or other electronic or mechanical methods, without the prior written permission of the publisher, except in the case of brief quotations embodied in critical reviews and specific other noncommercial uses permitted by copyright law.

Any references to historical events, real people, or real places are used fictitiously. Names, characters, and places are products of the author's imagination.

ISBN: 979-8-987-5023-6-5 (Paperback)

www.youthsuccesscoaching.org

Author

Sheryl Ellis is a mental health therapist, youth life coach, mentor, writer, and author of Christian-based books and curricula for youth. With over a decade of therapeutic youth services, Sheryl has a voice that shines through in her newest collection of books, exploring the importance of youth social and emotional wellness. Sheryl has a BA in Psychology and an MA in marriage and family counseling and is currently completing a PH. D in Developmental Psychology. Sheryl is a certified (TF-CBT) Trauma Focused Cognitive Behavioral Therapist working in schools, hospitals, and behavioral health centers, providing therapy for severely at-risk youth and teens. When not providing therapeutic services, Sheryl loves cooking, swimming, mountain bike riding, camping, and spending time with her family.

Table of Contents

Introduction	9
Resilience and Coping Skills Training Manual	12
Resilience and Coping Skills	33
Life Purpose Course Manual	78
Life Purpose Course	91
Empowerment for Youth Course Manual	116
Empowerment for Youth Course	128
Key Note	173

Introduction

About Integrating Mental Health & Life Coaching

I am thrilled to introduce "***Integrating Mental Health & Life Coaching***," a comprehensive coaching course designed to equip parents, guardians, and trusted adults with the tools to support the youth in their care. Today's young people face various challenges—social pressures, academic stress, and personal struggles—and it can often be challenging to know how best to help them navigate these obstacles, develop resilience, and ultimately thrive. Our self-paced course on *Life Purpose, Empowerment, Resiliency, and Coping Skills* offers a solution, providing a structured framework to guide youth through critical areas of personal growth and mental health.

Overview:

This 8-week program will help you empower youth by fostering resilience, self-awareness, and goal setting. The course includes practical exercises that develop essential coping skills, emotional intelligence, and personal growth strategies. With every lesson, youth will be encouraged to tap into their inner strength, build confidence, and discover a sense of purpose, all while developing practical tools to thrive in today's world.

A well-structured *teaching manual* accompanies the three programs, ensuring you have everything you need to confidently lead youth through empowerment, personal growth, and emotional resilience lessons. You'll walk alongside them as they explore critical life skills, from understanding their emotions to setting goals and developing healthy coping mechanisms.

The program covers the following key areas:

1. **Universal Teaching Manual:** Designed to guide parents, guardians, and trusted adults in helping youth work through the material.
2. **Early Weeks:** Youth are introduced to fundamental concepts such as the *Stages of Change* and *Love Languages*, helping them gain better insight into personal transformation and fostering deeper emotional connections. They will also explore the importance of a *Growth Mindset*, learning to view challenges as opportunities for growth rather than obstacles.
3. **Gratitude Practices:** As the course progresses, you will guide youth through powerful gratitude exercises to foster emotional resilience. They will keep a *Gratitude Journal*, participate in daily reflection exercises, and learn how expressing gratitude can positively impact their mindset and outlook.
4. **Personal Narratives and Visualization:** In later weeks, youth will reflect on their narratives—past, present, and future—and explore visualization techniques to help them picture their *Best Possible Self.* These exercises will help them shape their identity, visualize their future, and align their actions with personal goals.
5. **Goal-Setting and SMART Goals:** The course culminates in goal-setting exercises where youth learn to create *SMART Goals* (Specific, Measurable, Achievable, Relevant, and Time-bound). These activities help youth focus on short-term and long-term aspirations, empowering them with the tools to turn their vision into concrete action plans.

This course goes beyond merely helping youth cope with life's difficulties—it empowers them to thrive by embracing their strengths, clarifying their vision, and taking confident, purposeful steps toward a fulfilling future. You will also learn how to support them in building robust support systems, from family to community networks, as part of their overall personal development journey.

With actionable tasks, relatable real-life examples, and a focus on practical growth, this course ensures you are equipped to help youth overcome adversity, build resilience, and unlock their full potential. Whether you are guiding a child, adolescent, or teen, *Integrating Mental Health & Life Coaching* provides the resources to make a meaningful impact on their lives.

Transform how you support the young people in your life today—this program will give you everything you need to ensure they emerge more robust, focused, and ready to thrive with a more profound sense of purpose. Together, let's make a difference in the next generation's lives.

Thank you for considering "***Integrating Mental Health & Life Coaching***." Together, let's make a difference in the lives of our children.

Key Note:

Any references to historical events, real people, or places are fictitious. Names, characters, and places are products of the author's imagination.

Building Resilience and Coping Skills for Youth Manual

This course is designed for parents, guardians, and trusted adults to help young people develop resilience and practical coping skills. It provides a comprehensive framework to understand and support the youth through various stages of their development. The course emphasizes practical strategies to nurture resilience, manage stress, and handle conflicts.

Course Objectives:
1. Understand the concept of resilience and its importance in youth development.
2. Learn about the locus of control and how it affects young people's perceptions of their abilities.
3. Identify and cultivate protective factors and social supports that enhance resilience.
4. Recognize stress symptoms and develop effective stress management techniques.
5. Develop problem-solving and conflict-resolution skills.
6. Encourage healthy coping mechanisms and time management skills.
7. Foster a supportive environment that promotes self-esteem and personal growth.

Weekly Introductions

Week 1: The Stages of Change, Love Language(s), Your Life Story, and a Satisfaction

Assessment

Introduction: This week introduces the concept of the stages of change and how understanding them can help guide youth through various challenges. We'll also explore love languages and their impact on relationships, reflect on personal life stories, and conduct a satisfaction assessment.

Key Areas:
- Stages of Change
- Love Languages
- Personal Life Stories
- Satisfaction Assessment

Week 2: Self-Esteem & Identification of Your Strengths

Introduction: Building self-esteem and recognizing personal strengths are crucial for resilience. This week focuses on strategies to enhance self-esteem and help youth identify and leverage their strengths.

Key Areas:
- Self-Esteem
- Personal Strengths

Week 3: Protective Factors, Social Supports, Locus of Control, and Your Tolerations

Introduction: Understanding protective factors and social supports helps create a supportive environment for youth. We'll also delve into the locus of control and how it influences perceptions and behaviors.

Key Areas:
- Protective Factors
- Social Supports
- Locus of Control
- Tolerations

Week 4: Stress Awareness, Stress Symptoms, Stress Management, and Relaxation Tips

Introduction: This week covers the nature of stress, its symptoms, and practical stress management techniques. We'll also discuss relaxation tips to help youth manage stress effectively.

Key Areas:
- Stress Awareness
- Stress Symptoms
- Stress Management
- Relaxation Tips

Week 5: Fight or Flight Response, Unhealthy Coping Skills, and Problem Solving

Introduction: Understanding the fight or flight response and identifying unhealthy coping skills are essential for effective problem-solving. This week provides tools to develop healthy problem-solving strategies.

Key Areas:
- Fight or Flight Response
- Unhealthy Coping Skills
- Problem-Solving

Week 6: Healthy Coping Skills, Tolerance Skills, and Self-Control

Introduction: This week focuses on developing healthy coping skills, tolerance, and self-control. These skills are critical for managing emotions and stress effectively.

Key Areas:
- Healthy Coping Skills
- Tolerance Skills

- Self-Control

Week 7: Peer Relationships, Conflict Resolutions, Bullies, and Time Management

Introduction: Effective peer relationships and conflict resolution are vital for youth. This week addresses strategies for handling bullying and managing time effectively.

Key Areas:
- Peer Relationships
- Conflict Resolutions
- Bullies
- Time Management

Week 8: Self-Care Tips, Positive Steps for Wellbeing, and Final Self-Care Assessment

Introduction: The final week emphasizes the importance of self-care and provides positive steps for maintaining well-being. We'll also conduct a final self-care assessment.

Key Areas:
- Self-Care Tips
- Positive Steps for Wellbeing
- Final Self-Care Assessment

Conclusion:
By the end of this course, parents, guardians, and trusted adults will be equipped with the knowledge and tools to support the youth in developing resilience and practical coping skills. This will help young people navigate life's challenges with confidence and strength.

Examples of Resilience and Coping Skills in Youth

Child (Ages 5-10)

Story Overview: Sophia, a 7-year-old, struggled with anxiety when starting a new school.

> Experiences: Sophia felt nervous and overwhelmed in her new environment, leading to frequent outbursts and withdrawal from activities.
>
> Overcoming Barriers: With her parents' support, Sophia practiced deep breathing exercises and used positive affirmations to manage her anxiety.
>
> Role of Parents/Guardians: Sophia's parents played a crucial role by maintaining open communication, encouraging her efforts, and seeking professional support when needed.
>
> Skills, Questions, and Tasks:
> - Locus of Control: Discuss with Sophia how she can control her reactions to new situations.
> - Success: Celebrate small achievements, like making a new friend.
> - Gratitude: Create a gratitude journal together.
> - Toleration: Help Sophia understand and tolerate her feelings of anxiety.
> - Time Management: Create a daily routine to provide structure.
> - Protective Factors: Identify trusted adults at school.
> - Stages of Change: Recognize and support Sophia's progress through her adjustment.

- Social Supports: Arrange playdates to build friendships.
- Understanding Stress: Teach Sophia to identify signs of stress.
- Problem Solving: Role-play different scenarios to practice coping strategies.
- Coping Skills: Practice deep breathing and mindfulness.
- Conflict Resolution: Discuss ways to handle conflicts with classmates.

Adolescent (Ages 11-14)

Story Overview: Liam, a 13-year-old, faced bullying at school, which affected his self-esteem.

Experiences: Liam became withdrawn, and his academic performance declined.

Overcoming Barriers: Liam learned assertiveness skills and sought help from school counselors.

Role of Parents/Guardians: Liam's parents advocated for him at school and provided emotional support at home.

Skills, Questions, and Tasks:
- Locus of Control: Encourage Liam to focus on actions he can control.
- Success: Recognize his strengths and accomplishments.
- Gratitude: Keep a gratitude list together.
- Toleration: Discuss ways to tolerate and manage stress.
- Time Management: Help Liam prioritize tasks and set goals.

- Protective Factors: Identify supportive peers and adults.
- Stages of Change: Guide Liam through the stages of addressing bullying.
- Social Supports: Strengthen his network of friends and mentors.
- Understanding Stress: Help Liam recognize stress triggers.
- Problem Solving: Develop strategies to address bullying.
- Coping Skills: Practice relaxation techniques and positive self-talk.
- Conflict Resolution: Role-play scenarios to practice assertiveness.

Teen (Ages 15-18)

Story Overview: Emma, a 17-year-old, struggled with academic pressure and social expectations.

Experiences: Emma experienced high levels of stress, leading to burnout.

Overcoming Barriers: Emma implemented time management strategies and sought support from friends and family.

Role of Parents/Guardians: Emma's parents provided a balanced perspective, encouraging breaks and extracurricular activities.

Skills, Questions, and Tasks:
- Locus of Control: Discuss Emma's influence over her academic choices.
- Success: Celebrate academic and personal achievements.

- Gratitude: Reflect on positive aspects of her life.
- Toleration: Help Emma tolerate and manage academic pressure.
- Time Management: Create a study schedule with breaks.
- Protective Factors: Identify mentors and supportive friends.
- Stages of Change: Support Emma's process of managing stress.
- Social Supports: Strengthen her support network.
- Understanding Stress: Teach Emma to recognize signs of burnout.
- Problem Solving: Develop strategies for academic challenges.
- Coping Skills: Practice mindfulness and exercise.
- Conflict Resolution: Discuss ways to handle conflicts with peers and teachers.

Overall Conclusion:

This course provides a comprehensive framework for parents, guardians, and trusted adults to support youth in developing resilience and practical coping skills. By understanding and implementing these strategies, adults can help young people navigate challenges and build a strong foundation for their future well-being.

Week-by-Week Lessons

Week 1: The Stages of Change, Love Language(s), Your Life Story, and a Satisfaction Assessment

Objective: To understand the stages of change, recognize love languages, reflect on personal life stories, and conduct a satisfaction assessment.

Lesson Plan:

Introduction:
- Discuss the importance of change and how it impacts our lives.
- Introduce the concept of love languages and how they affect relationships.

Stages of Change:
- Explain the five stages of change: pre-contemplation, Contemplation, Preparation, Action, and Maintenance.
- Discuss how understanding these stages can help support youth in their personal growth.

Love Languages:
- Introduce the five love languages: Words of Affirmation, Acts of Service, Receiving Gifts, Quality Time, and Physical Touch.
- Have participants take a quiz to identify their primary love language and discuss the results.

Your Life Story:
- Encourage participants to share their life stories, focusing on significant events and how they have shaped their current selves.

- Discuss how reflecting on personal experiences can provide insights into current behaviors and attitudes.

Satisfaction Assessment:
- Guide participants through a satisfaction assessment in various life areas (e.g., family, school, social life, hobbies).
- Discuss the results and identify areas for potential improvement.

Tasks:
- Reflect on a recent change and identify which stage you were in.
- Discuss your love language with a trusted adult or friend and find ways to express it in your relationships.
- Write a brief autobiography highlighting critical events in your life.
- Complete a satisfaction assessment and identify two areas to focus on for improvement.

Questions:
- How do you typically respond to change?
- What is your primary love language, and how can you use it to improve your relationships?
- How have significant life events shaped who you are today?
- Which areas of your life are you most satisfied with? Which needs more attention?

Week 2: Self-Esteem & Identification of Your Strengths

Objective: To build self-esteem and identify strengths that can be leveraged for personal growth and resilience.

Lesson Plan:

Introduction:
- Discuss the importance of self-esteem and how it affects overall well-being.

Building Self-Esteem:
- Explore factors influencing self-esteem (e.g., family, friends, school, media).
- Discuss practical ways to boost self-esteem, such as positive affirmations and self-compassion.

Identifying Personal Strengths:
- Conduct a strengths assessment (e.g., VIA Character Strengths Survey).
- Discuss how recognizing and using personal strengths can enhance self-esteem and resilience.

Activities:
- Create a "Strengths and Achievements" journal to document personal strengths and accomplishments.
- Practice positive affirmations daily and reflect on the impact.

Tasks:
- Identify three strengths you possess and write about how you can use them daily.
- List five positive affirmations and practice saying them every day.
- Reflect on a time when you used one of your strengths to overcome a challenge.

Questions:
- What are your top three strengths?
- How can you use your strengths to improve your self-esteem?
- What positive affirmations resonate with you?
- How do you feel when focusing on your strengths instead of your weaknesses?

Week 3: Protective Factors, Social Supports, Locus of Control, and Your Tolerations

Objective: To understand protective factors and social supports, explore the concept of locus of control, and identify personal tolerations.

Lesson Plan:

Introduction:
- Discuss how protective factors and social supports contribute to resilience.

Protective Factors:
- Identify protective factors that support resilience, such as positive relationships, supportive environments, and healthy coping skills.

Social Supports:
- Discuss the importance of social support networks and how to build and maintain them.

Locus of Control:
- Explain the difference between internal and external locus of control.

- Discuss how having an internal locus of control can enhance resilience and coping skills.

Your Tolerations:
- Define tolerations and discuss how they can impact well-being.
- Encourage participants to identify and address their tolerations.

Activities:
- Create a map of your social support network and identify key people who provide support.
- Reflect on situations where you demonstrated an internal locus of control.
- List tolerations in your life and create a plan to address them.

Tasks:
- Identify three protective factors in your life and discuss how they help you.
- Map out your social support network.
- Reflect on your locus of control and identify areas where you can take more control.
- List five tolerations and develop a plan to address them.

Questions:
- What protective factors do you have in your life?
- Who are the key people in your social support network?
- Do you tend to have an internal or external locus of control? How does this affect you?
- What are some tolerations in your life, and how can you address them?

Week 4: Stress Awareness, Stress Symptoms, Stress Management, and Relaxation Tips

Objective: To raise awareness about stress, recognize stress symptoms, and develop effective stress management and relaxation techniques.

Lesson Plan:

Introduction:
- Discuss the nature of stress and its impact on physical and mental health.

Stress Awareness:
- Explain the causes of stress and how it manifests in different individuals.

Stress Symptoms:
- Identify common physical, emotional, and behavioral symptoms of stress.

Stress Management:
- Discuss various stress management techniques, such as exercise, mindfulness, and time management.

Relaxation Tips:
- Introduce relaxation techniques like deep breathing, progressive muscle relaxation, and visualization.

Activities:
- Practice deep breathing and progressive muscle relaxation.
- Create a stress management plan incorporating preferred techniques.

Tasks:
- Identify personal stressors and reflect on how they affect you.
- Practice at least one relaxation technique daily and journal your experience.
- Develop a stress management plan tailored to your needs.

Questions:
- What are your primary sources of stress?
- How does stress affect you physically, emotionally, and behaviorally?
- Which stress management techniques work best for you?
- How can you incorporate relaxation into your daily routine?

Week 5: Fight or Flight Response, Unhealthy Coping Skills, and Problem Solving

Objective: To understand the fight or flight response, recognize unhealthy coping skills, and develop effective problem-solving strategies.
Lesson Plan:

Introduction:
- Discuss the fight or flight response and its evolutionary purpose.

Fight or Flight Response:
- Please explain how the fight or flight response is triggered and its effects on the body.

Unhealthy Coping Skills:
- Identify common unhealthy coping mechanisms (e.g., avoidance, substance use, aggression) and their impact.

Problem Solving:
- Introduce a problem-solving framework (e.g., identifying the problem, brainstorming solutions, evaluating options, implementing a plan, and reviewing the outcome).

Activities:
- Role-play scenarios to practice healthy problem-solving strategies.
- Reflect on past situations where unhealthy coping skills were used and brainstorm healthier alternatives.

Tasks:
- Identify situations that trigger your fight or flight response.
- Reflect on any unhealthy coping skills you use and their impact.
- Practice the problem-solving framework with a current issue you are facing.

Questions:
- How does the fight or flight response manifest in you?
- What are some unhealthy coping skills you tend to use?
- How can you replace unhealthy coping mechanisms with healthier ones?
- What steps can you take to solve problems effectively?

Week 6: Healthy Coping Skills, Tolerance Skills, and Self-Control

Objective: To develop healthy coping skills, tolerance skills, and self-control.

Lesson Plan:

Introduction:
- Discuss the importance of healthy coping skills and self-control in managing stress and emotions.

Healthy Coping Skills:
- Identify and practice healthy coping mechanisms like exercise, hobbies, and social activities.

Tolerance Skills:
- Discuss strategies to build tolerance for stress and discomfort.

Self-Control:
- Explore techniques for developing self-control, such as mindfulness and delayed gratification.

Activities:
- Practice mindfulness meditation.
- Create a list of healthy coping activities to use in times of stress.

Tasks:
- Identify three healthy coping skills you can use regularly.
- Reflect on situations where you successfully used self-control.
- Develop a plan to build tolerance for a specific stressor in your life.

Questions:
- What are your go-to healthy coping skills?
- How do you build tolerance for stress and discomfort?
- What strategies help you maintain self-control?
- How can you practice self-control in challenging situations?

Week 7: Peer Relationships, Conflict Resolutions, Bullies, and Time Management

Objective: To improve peer relationships, develop conflict resolution skills, address bullying, and enhance time management skills.

Lesson Plan:

Introduction:
- Discuss the importance of healthy peer relationships and effective time management.

Peer Relationships:
- Explore strategies for building and maintaining positive peer relationships.

Conflict Resolution:
- Introduce conflict resolution techniques, such as active listening, empathy, and finding common ground.

Addressing Bullies:
- Discuss strategies for dealing with bullying, including seeking help and assertive communication.

Time Management:
- Explore time management techniques, such as prioritization, scheduling, and setting goals.

Activities:
- Role-play conflict resolution scenarios.
- Create a weekly schedule to improve time management.

Tasks:
- Identify qualities of healthy peer relationships.
- Reflect on a past conflict and how it was resolved.
- Develop a plan to address any bullying situations.
- Create a time management plan for the upcoming week.

Questions:
- What qualities make a good friend?
- How can you effectively resolve conflicts with peers?
- What steps can you take to address bullying?
- How can you improve your time management skills?

Week 8: Self-Care Tips, Positive Steps for Wellbeing, and Final Self-Care Assessment

Objective: To emphasize the importance of self-care and provide practical steps for maintaining well-being.

Lesson Plan:

Introduction:
- Discuss the role of self-care in overall well-being and resilience.

Self-Care Tips:
- Explore various self-care activities, such as exercise, hobbies, and relaxation.

Positive Steps for Wellbeing:
- Identify steps to enhance physical, mental, and emotional well-being.

Final Self-Care Assessment:
- Conduct a final self-care assessment to reflect on progress and identify areas for continued growth.

Activities:
- Create a personalized self-care plan.
- Reflect on progress made during the course.

Tasks:
- Identify three self-care activities you can incorporate into your routine.
- Reflect on positive changes you've made in your well-being.
- Complete the final self-care assessment and set goals for the future.

Questions:
- What self-care activities help you feel your best?
- How can you continue to prioritize self-care in your life?
- What positive steps have you taken for your well-being?
- What goals do you have for maintaining and improving your self-care routine?

Overall Conclusion

By completing this course, parents, guardians, and trusted adults will be equipped with the knowledge and tools to support youth in developing resilience and practical coping skills. Through understanding key concepts, engaging in practical activities, and reflecting on personal experiences, adults can help young people navigate life's challenges with confidence and strength.

Resilience and Coping Skills for Kids:

A Fun and Engaging Course

Week 1: Understanding Change, Love Languages, and Your Story

Objective: To understand the change process, discover love languages, and reflect on personal life stories.

Activities:

Stages of Change

- Game: "Change Adventure Bingo"
    - Materials Needed: Bingo cards with five stages of change (pre-contemplation, Contemplation, Preparation, Action, Maintenance) and examples, markers, or chips.
    - How to Play:
        - Create a bingo card with a 5x5 grid. Each column represents a stage of change, and each cell contains an example (e.g., "Thinking about starting a new hobby" for Contemplation).
        - The facilitator reads out scenarios related to changes.
        - Kids mark off the corresponding stage on their bingo cards.
        - The first to get five in a row (vertical, horizontal, or diagonal) shouts "Bingo!" and wins a small prize.
    - Duration: 20-30 minutes

Your Life Story

- Storytime: "My Life Adventure Map"
    - Materials Needed: Large sheets of paper (A3 size or larger), colored markers, crayons or pencils, and stickers (optional).
    - How to Create:
        - Draw a big, curvy road on the paper. This road represents your life journey.
        - Along the road, draw pictures or use stickers to mark important events and milestones (e.g., first day of school, family vacation, learning to ride a bike).
        - Add dates, ages, or years to each event.
        - Use different colors to show how you felt during those times.
    - Sharing:
        - Break into pairs.
        - Each person has 5 minutes to share their map with their partner.
    - Duration: 40 minutes (20 for creation, 20 for sharing)
- Show and Tell
    - Preparation: Bring a particular object from home that reminds you of an essential time in your life.
    - How to Share:
        - Sit in a circle.
        - Each person has 2 minutes to show their object and explain why it's unique and what it represents.
    - Duration: 30 minutes (for a group of 15)

Reflection

- Journal: "My Changes" Notebook
    - Materials Needed: Journals or notepads, pens/pencils.
    - Writing Prompts:
        1. Describe a recent change you experienced. What happened?
        2. How did this change make you feel? List at least three emotions.
        3. What helped you deal with this change?
    - Sharing:
        - If you want, you can share what you wrote with the group.
    - Duration: 15 minutes of writing, 10 minutes optional sharing

Questions

- Discussion Questions:
    1. What was a significant change you went through recently?
    2. What's your love language, and how can you use it with your friends and family?
    3. What's a critical event in your life story?
- Duration: Allocate 5 minutes per question for group discussion.

This detailed breakdown provides explicit instructions, materials needed, and time allocations for each activity, making it easy to implement and ensuring a comprehensive exploration of the topics.

Week 2: Building Self-Esteem and Finding Your Strengths

Objective: To boost self-esteem and identify personal strengths.

Activities:

Self-Esteem Building

Mirror Affirmations

- Activity: Stand in front of a mirror and say five positive things about yourself.
- Materials Needed: A mirror, sticky notes, and a pen.
- Instructions:
    - Each child stands in front of a mirror.
    - They say five positive affirmations about themselves (e.g., "I am kind," "I am smart," "I am a good friend").
    - Write each affirmation on a sticky note and place it around the mirror.
    - Encourage kids to repeat these affirmations daily.
- Duration: 10-15 minutes

Self-Esteem Tree

- Activity: Draw a tree and write positive qualities about yourself on the leaves.
- Materials Needed: Large sheets of paper, colored markers, crayons, or pencils.
- Instructions:
    - Draw a large tree with branches and leaves.
    - On each leaf, write a positive quality or something you like about yourself (e.g., "I am creative," "I am helpful").
    - Decorate the tree with colors and stickers.

- Display the trees in the classroom or home as a reminder of their positive qualities.
- Duration: 20-30 minutes

Additional Self-Esteem Building Activities

Compliment Circle

- Activity: Sit in a circle and compliment each other.
- Materials Needed: None.
- Instructions:
  - Sit in a circle.
  - Each child takes a turn complimenting the person next to them.
  - Continue until everyone has received and given a compliment.
- Duration: 15-20 minutes

Positive Jar

- Activity: Create a jar filled with positive notes.
- Materials Needed: A jar, small pieces of paper, pens/pencils.
- Instructions:
  - Write positive notes about yourself or others on small pieces of paper.
  - Fold the notes and place them in the jar.
  - They can take a note from the jar whenever someone needs a boost.
- Duration: 15-20 minutes

Identifying Strengths

Strengths Hunt

- Activity: Go on a scavenger hunt around your house or classroom to find items representing your strengths.
- Materials Needed: Scavenger hunt list, bags, or baskets for collecting items.
- Instructions:
    - Create a list of strengths (e.g., creativity, kindness, problem-solving).
    - Find items around the house or classroom representing each strength (e.g., a paintbrush for creativity or a book for knowledge).
    - Share the items and explain how they represent your strengths.
- Duration: 30-40 minutes

Superhero Poster

- Activity: Create a poster of yourself as a superhero, highlighting your unique strengths.
- Materials Needed: Large sheets of paper, colored markers, crayons, pencils, stickers, and magazines for cutouts.
- Instructions:
    - Draw yourself as a superhero on a large sheet of paper.
    - Add details like a superhero name, costume, and special powers.
    - Write or draw your unique strengths and qualities around the superhero.
    - Decorate the poster with stickers and cutouts from magazines.
    - Display the posters in the classroom or at home.
- Duration: 30-40 minutes

Additional Strengths Identification Activities

Strengths Collage

- Activity: Create a collage that represents your strengths.
- Materials Needed: Magazines, scissors, glue, large sheets of paper.
- Instructions:
    - Cut out pictures and words from magazines that represent your strengths.
    - Glue them onto a large sheet of paper to create a collage.
    - Share your collage with the group and explain your choices.
- Duration: 30-40 minutes

Strengths Bracelet

- Activity: Make a bracelet with beads representing your strengths.
- Materials Needed: Beads in different colors, elastic cord or string, scissors.
- Instructions:
    - Choose beads representing your strengths (e.g., blue for calmness, red for courage).
    - String the beads onto the cord and tie it off to make a bracelet.
    - Wear the bracelet as a reminder of your strengths.
- Duration: 20-30 minutes

These expanded activities provide various engaging and creative ways for kids to build self-esteem and identify their strengths, fostering a positive self-image and confidence.

Reflection:

- Journal: Write about a time when you felt proud of yourself.

Questions:

- What are three things you like about yourself?
- What strengths make you unique?
- When did you last feel proud of something you did?

Week 3: Finding Your Support Network and Understanding Control

Objective: Identify supportive people and understand what you can control.

Activities:

Support Network

Support Circle

- Activity: Draw a big circle and write the names of people who support you inside the circle.
- Materials Needed: Large sheets of paper, colored markers, or pencils.
- Instructions:
    1. Draw a large circle on the paper.
    2. In the center, write your name or draw a picture of yourself.
    3. Around you, write names or draw pictures of people who support you (family, friends, teachers, etc.).

4. Use different colors to categorize types of support (e.g., blue for emotional support and green for practical help).
5. Add small symbols next to each name to represent how they support you (e.g., a heart for love, a book for advice).
- Duration: 20-25 minutes

Role Play

- Activity: Act out scenarios where you ask for help from your support network.
- Materials Needed: Scenario cards, props (optional).
- Instructions:
    1. Create cards with different scenarios (e.g., "You're having trouble with homework," "You're feeling sad and need to talk").
    2. Divide into small groups.
    3. Each group draws a scenario card and acts out how to ask for help from their support network.
    4. Discuss practical ways to communicate needs and ask for support.
- Duration: 30-40 minutes

Additional Support Network Activities

Support Web

- Activity: Create a visual web of connections in your support network.
- Materials Needed: Ball of yarn, scissors.
- Instructions:
    1. Stand in a circle.
    2. One person starts with the yarn and names someone who supports them.

3. They pass the yarn to that person while holding onto a piece.
4. Continue until everyone is connected to the web.
5. Discuss how the web represents strength in connections.
- Duration: 15-20 minutes

Gratitude Letters

- Activity: Write thank-you letters to members of your support network.
- Materials Needed: Paper, envelopes, pens, decorative materials.
- Instructions:
    1. Choose someone from your support network.
    2. Please write a letter expressing gratitude for their support.
    3. Decorate the letter and envelope.
    4. Share letters with the group (optional) and deliver them to recipients.
- Duration: 25-30 minutes

Locus of Control

Control Jar

- Activity: Decorate a jar and fill it with slips of paper with things you can control written on them.
- Materials Needed: Clear jars, decorative materials (stickers, ribbons, paint), small slips of paper, and pens.
- Instructions:
    1. Decorate the outside of your jar.
    2. On slips of paper, write things you can control (e.g., "My attitude," "How I treat others").
    3. Fill the jar with these slips.

        4. Create a second set of slips with things you can't control, discuss these, then discard them.
        5. Keep the jar as a reminder to focus on what you can control.
- Duration: 30-35 minutes

Control Comic Strip

- Activity: Create a comic strip showing a character dealing with a problem by focusing on what they can control.
- Materials Needed: Comic strip templates, pencils, and colored markers.
- Instructions:
    1. Choose a problem scenario (e.g., "It's raining on a planned outdoor day").
    2. Create a 4-6 panel comic strip showing:
        - The problem
        - The character's initial reaction
        - The character identifies what they can and can't control
        - The character taking action on what they can control
        - The positive outcome
    3. Share comics with the group and discuss strategies used.
- Duration: 35-45 minutes

Additional Locus of Control Activities

Control vs. Influence Sorting Game

- Activity: Sort situations into categories of "Can Control," "Can Influence," and "Can't Control."
- Materials Needed: Cards with various situations, three labeled boxes.

- Instructions:
    1. Create cards with different situations (e.g., "The weather," "Your homework completion").
    2. Sort the cards into the appropriate boxes.
    3. Discuss why each situation belongs in its category.
    4. Focus on strategies for situations you can control or influence.
- Duration: 20-25 minutes

"I Can" Affirmation Flags

- Activity: Create small flags with "I Can" statements about things you can control.
- Materials Needed: Colored paper, popsicle sticks, markers, glue.
- Instructions:
    1. Cut paper into small flag shapes.
    2. Write "I Can" statements on each flag (e.g., "I can choose to be kind").
    3. Decorate the flags and attach them to popsicle sticks.
    4. Display the flags in a prominent place as reminders.
- Duration: 25-30 minutes

These expanded activities provide engaging and interactive ways for children to understand and strengthen their support networks and develop a healthy locus of control. They encourage reflection, creativity, and practical application of these essential concepts.

Reflection:

- Journal: Write about a time when you asked for help, and it improved things.

Questions:

- Who are the people in your support circle?
- What are some things you can control in your life?
- How does it feel to ask for help when you need it?

Week 4: Recognizing and Managing Stress

Objective: To understand stress and learn ways to manage it.

Activities:

Stress Awareness

Stress Ball DIY

- Activity: Make your stress ball using a balloon, rice, or flour.
- Materials Needed: Balloons, rice or flour, funnels, scissors, and permanent markers.
- Instructions:
    1. Use a funnel to fill a balloon with rice or flour.
    2. Tie off the balloon and cut off any excess.
    3. Draw a face or design on the balloon with permanent markers.
    4. Discuss how squeezing the stress ball can help release tension.
- Duration: 20-25 minutes

Stress Monsters

- Activity: Draw or create little monsters that represent different stressors you face.
- Materials Needed: Paper, colored markers or crayons, craft supplies (optional: googly eyes, pipe cleaners, pom-poms).
- Instructions:
    1. Identify different stressors (e.g., tests, arguments with friends).
    2. Draw or create a monster for each stressor.
    3. Name each monster and describe its "powers" (how it makes you feel).
    4. Discuss strategies to "defeat" each stress monster.
- Duration: 30-35 minutes

Additional Stress Awareness Activities

Stress Body Map

- Activity: Create a body outline and color areas where you feel stress.
- Materials Needed: Large paper, colored markers, or crayons.
- Instructions:
    1. Trace a body outline on large paper.
    2. Use different colors to show where you feel stress in your body (e.g., red for headaches, blue for stomach aches).
    3. Discuss common stress symptoms and healthy ways to address them.
- Duration: 25-30 minutes

Stress Weather Report

- Activity: Create a personal "weather report" to describe your stress levels.
- Materials Needed: Paper, colored markers, weather symbols (sun, clouds, rain, storm).
- Instructions:
    1. Draw or use weather symbols to represent different stress levels.
    2. Create a weekly "forecast" of your expected stress levels.
    3. Discuss what causes "stormy" days and how to create more "sunny" days.
- Duration: 20-25 minutes

Stress Management

Breathing Exercises

- Activity: Practice deep breathing by blowing bubbles and watching them float away.
- Materials Needed: Bubble solution, bubble wands.
- Instructions:
    1. Demonstrate slow, deep breathing.
    2. Practice blowing bubbles with controlled breath.
    3. Imagine stress floating away with each bubble.
    4. Discuss how deep breathing can help calm the mind and body.
- Duration: 15-20 minutes

Calm Jar

- Activity: Create a quiet jar filled with glitter and water to shake and watch when you need to relax.
- Materials Needed: Clear jars with lids, glitter, water, glycerin or clear glue, and food coloring (optional).

- Instructions:
    1. Fill jars 3/4 full with warm water.
    2. Add glitter and a few drops of food coloring.
    3. Add a tablespoon of glycerin or clear glue to slow the glitter's fall.
    4. Seal the jar tightly.
    5. Shake the jar and watch the glitter settle, focusing on deep breathing.
- Duration: 25-30 minutes

Additional Stress Management Activities

Mindful Minute

- Activity: Practice one-minute mindfulness exercises.
- Materials Needed: Timer, various sensory items (e.g., feathers, smooth stones, scented oils).
- Instructions:
    1. Set a timer for one minute.
    2. Focus on a single sense (sight, sound, touch, smell) for the full minute.
    3. Discuss how being present in the moment can reduce stress.
- Duration: 15-20 minutes (including multiple rounds)

Worry Box

- Activity: Create a box to "store" worries and concerns.
- Materials Needed: Small boxes, decorative materials, paper, pens.
- Instructions:
    1. Decorate a small box to be your "worry box."
    2. Write down worries on slips of paper.
    3. Place the worries in the box.
    4. Set a specific "worry time" to address concerns in the box.

5. Discuss how this can help manage intrusive thoughts throughout the day.
- Duration: 30-35 minutes

Stress-Relief Playlist

- Activity: Create a playlist of calming or uplifting songs.
- Materials Needed: Devices with music apps, headphones, paper, pens.
- Instructions:
    1. Brainstorm songs that help you feel calm or happy.
    2. Create a playlist on a music app or write down the song list.
    3. Share favorite calming songs with the group.
    4. Discuss how music can influence mood and reduce stress.
- Duration: 25-30 minutes

These expanded activities provide various engaging and interactive ways for children to become aware of their stress and learn effective stress management techniques. They encourage creativity, self-reflection, and the development of practical coping skills.

Reflection:

- Journal: Write about when you felt stressed and what helped you feel better.

Questions:

- What are some things that make you feel stressed?
- How can you use your calm jar or stress ball to relax?
- What helps you feel better when you're stressed?

Week 5: Dealing with Big Feelings and Solving Problems

Objective: To understand the fight or flight response, recognize unhealthy coping skills, and learn problem-solving techniques.

Activities:

Fight or Flight

Reaction Time Game

- Activity: Play a game that tests your reaction time to understand how quick reactions work.
- Materials: Online reaction time test or physical objects for a real-world test.
- Instructions:
    1. Use an online reaction time test or set up a physical test (e.g., catching a dropped ruler).
    2. Record reaction times for each participant.
    3. Discuss how stress might affect reaction times.
- Duration: 15-20 minutes

Feeling Faces

- Activity: Draw faces showing different emotions you feel in fight or flight mode.
- Materials: Paper, colored pencils, or markers.
- Instructions:
    1. Discuss common emotions during a fight or flight (fear, anger, anxiety).
    2. Draw faces expressing these emotions.
    3. Share drawings and discuss physical sensations associated with each emotion.
- Duration: 20-25 minutes

Additional Fight or Flight Activities

Body Map

- Activity: Create a body outline and mark areas affected during fight or flight.
- Materials: Large paper, markers.
- Instructions:
    1. Trace a body outline on large paper.
    2. Mark areas affected during stress (e.g., racing heart, sweaty palms).
    3. Discuss physical responses and how to recognize them.
- Duration: 25-30 minutes

Freeze Dance

- Activity: Play freeze dance to practice quick reactions and stopping.
- Materials: Music player.
- Instructions:
    1. Play music and have kids dance.
    2. Randomly stop the music; kids must freeze immediately.
    3. Discuss how this relates to fight or flight responses.
- Duration: 15-20 minutes

Unhealthy Coping Skills

Coping Detective

- Activity: Be a detective and identify unhealthy coping skills in story characters or movies.
- Materials: Short stories or movie clips, detective hats (optional).

- Instructions:
    1. Read stories or watch clips featuring characters using coping skills.
    2. Identify and discuss unhealthy coping methods.
    3. Suggest healthier alternatives for the characters.
- Duration: 30-35 minutes

Coping Choice Board

- Activity: Create a board with healthy coping options when feeling stressed.
- Materials: Poster board, markers, stickers, magazines for cutouts.
- Instructions:
    1. Brainstorm healthy coping strategies.
    2. Create a colorful board with different coping choices.
    3. Categorize choices (e.g., physical activities, creative outlets, social support).
- Duration: 35-40 minutes

Additional Unhealthy Coping Skills Activities

Coping Skills Sorting Game

- Activity: Sort coping skills into "healthy" and "unhealthy" categories.
- Materials: Cards with various coping skills written on them, two boxes labeled "healthy" and "unhealthy."
- Instructions:
    1. Create cards with different coping strategies.
    2. Have kids sort the cards into the appropriate boxes.
    3. Discuss why each strategy is healthy or unhealthy.
- Duration: 20-25 minutes

Role-Play Scenarios

- Activity: Act out scenarios demonstrating healthy and unhealthy coping.
- Materials: Scenario cards.
- Instructions:
    1. Create cards with different stressful scenarios.
    2. In small groups, act out the scenario using healthy and unhealthy coping.
    3. Discuss the differences and consequences of each approach.
- Duration: 30-35 minutes

Problem-Solving

Problem-Solving Maze

- Activity: Navigate a maze where each turn represents a step in solving a problem.
- Materials: Large paper for drawing maze, markers.
- Instructions:
    1. Create a maze with decision points representing problem-solving steps.
    2. Have kids navigate the maze, explaining their choices at each turn.
    3. Discuss how different paths lead to different outcomes.
- Duration: 25-30 minutes

Solution Station

- Activity: Set up a station with different tools and steps for solving a problem.
- Materials: Various problem-solving tools (e.g., paper, pens, building blocks, puzzle pieces).
- Instructions:

1. Set up stations with different types of problems and tools.
2. Have kids rotate through stations, using tools to solve problems.
3. Discuss different approaches and strategies used.
- Duration: 35-40 minutes

Additional Problem-Solving Activities

Problem-Solving Charades

- Activity: Act out problem-solving steps without words.
- Materials: Cards with problem-solving steps written on them.
- Instructions:
    1. Create cards with steps like "Identify the problem," "Brainstorm solutions," etc.
    2. Have kids act out the steps while others guess.
    3. Discuss the importance of each step in problem-solving.
- Duration: 20-25 minutes

Build-a-Bridge Challenge

- Activity: Solve a practical problem by building a bridge with limited materials.
- Materials: Popsicle sticks, string, tape, small weights.
- Instructions:
    1. Challenge kids to build a bridge that can hold weight using limited materials.
    2. Encourage planning, testing, and revising strategies.
    3. Discuss how they approached the problem and what they learned.
- Duration: 40-45 minutes

These expanded activities provide various engaging and interactive ways for children to understand fight or flight responses, recognize unhealthy coping skills, and develop problem-solving abilities. They encourage critical thinking, creativity, and practical application of these essential concepts.

Reflection:

- Journal: Write about a problem you solved recently and how you did it.

Questions:

- How do you feel when you're in fight or flight mode?
- What are some unhealthy ways of coping with stress?
- How can you solve problems healthily?

Week 6: Learning Healthy Coping Skills and Self-Control

Objective: To develop healthy coping skills, tolerance skills, and self-control.

Activities:

Healthy Coping Skills

Coping Collage

- Activity: Create a collage of pictures and words representing healthy coping skills.
- Materials Needed: Magazines, scissors, glue, large sheets of paper, markers.
- Instructions:

    1. Discuss healthy coping skills (e.g., exercise, talking to a friend, reading).
    2. Cut out pictures and words from magazines that represent these coping skills.
    3. Glue the cutouts onto a large sheet of paper to create a collage.
    4. Share your collage with the group and explain your choices.
- Duration: 30-40 minutes

Mindfulness Walk

- Activity: Go on a walk and practice mindfulness by paying attention to the sights, sounds, and smells around you.
- Materials Needed: Comfortable walking shoes and a safe walking route.
- Instructions:
    1. Walk in a safe area (e.g., school grounds, park).
    2. Focus on being present and noticing the environment around you.
    3. Pay attention to the sights, sounds, and smells.
    4. After the walk, discuss how mindfulness can help reduce stress.
- Duration: 20-30 minutes

Additional Healthy Coping Skills Activities

Stress Relief Art

- Activity: Create art to express and manage stress.
- Materials Needed: Paper, paints, markers, crayons.
- Instructions:
    1. Use art supplies to create a piece of art that represents your feelings.

2. Focus on the process of creating rather than the final product.
   3. Share your artwork with the group and discuss how creating art can be a healthy coping skill.
- Duration: 30-40 minutes

Guided Imagery

- Activity: Practice guided imagery to relax and reduce stress.
- Materials Needed: Comfortable seating, a quiet space, and a script for guided imagery.
- Instructions:
   1. Sit comfortably in a quiet space.
   2. Listen to a guided imagery script or recording.
   3. Visualize the peaceful scenes described.
   4. Discuss how guided imagery made you feel and how it can be used as a coping skill.
- Duration: 15-20 minutes

Tolerance Skills

Tolerance Tower

- Activity: Build a tower using blocks, each representing something you're learning to tolerate.
- Materials Needed: Building blocks (e.g., LEGO, wooden blocks), markers.
- Instructions:
   1. Write different things you're learning to tolerate on the blocks (e.g., waiting, sharing, losing a game).
   2. Build a tower using these blocks.
   3. Discuss how each block represents a challenge and how building the tower symbolizes growing tolerance.

- Duration: 20-25 minutes

Patience Puzzle

- Activity: Complete a puzzle to practice patience and tolerance.
- Materials Needed: Age-appropriate puzzles.
- Instructions:
    1. Work on completing a puzzle individually or in small groups.
    2. Focus on being patient and working through challenges.
    3. Discuss how completing the puzzle required patience and tolerance.
- Duration: 30-40 minutes

Additional Tolerance Skills Activities

Tolerance Timeline

- Activity: Create a timeline of events where you had to practice tolerance.
- Materials Needed: Paper, markers, stickers.
- Instructions:
    1. Draw a timeline on a large sheet of paper.
    2. Mark events where you had to practice tolerance (e.g., waiting for a turn, dealing with a difficult situation).
    3. Decorate the timeline with stickers and drawings.
    4. Share your timeline with the group and discuss what you learned from each event.
- Duration: 25-30 minutes

Tolerance Role-Play

- Activity: Act out scenarios that require tolerance.
- Materials Needed: Scenario cards.
- Instructions:
    1. Create cards with different scenarios that require tolerance (e.g., waiting in line, sharing toys).
    2. In small groups, act out the scenarios.
    3. Discuss how to handle each situation with tolerance and patience.
- Duration: 30-35 minutes

Self-Control

Marshmallow Test

- Activity: Try the marshmallow test to practice delayed gratification.
- Materials Needed: Marshmallows or another treat, a timer.
- Instructions:
    1. Give each child a marshmallow and explain that they can eat it now or wait 10 minutes to get a second one.
    2. Set a timer for 10 minutes.
    3. Observe and discuss the choices made.
    4. Talk about the importance of delayed gratification and self-control.
- Duration: 15-20 minutes

Impulse Control Game

- Activity: Play a game like "Simon Says" to practice controlling impulses.
- Materials Needed: None.
- Instructions:

1. Play "Simon Says" with the group, giving commands that they should only follow if prefaced with "Simon says."
2. Discuss how the game helps practice listening and controlling impulses.
3. Reflect on how these skills can be used in everyday situations.
- Duration: 15-20 minutes

Additional Self-Control Activities

Self-Control Charades

- Activity: Act out scenarios requiring self-control without speaking.
- Materials Needed: Scenario cards.
- Instructions:
    1. Create cards with scenarios that require self-control (e.g., not interrupting, waiting your turn).
    2. Act out the scenarios while others guess what is being demonstrated.
    3. Discuss the importance of self-control in each scenario.
- Duration: 20-25 minutes

Self-Control Journal

- Activity: Keep a journal to track moments of self-control.
- Materials Needed: Journals or notebooks, pens.
- Instructions:
    1. Write about times when you practiced self-control during the day.
    2. Reflect on what made it challenging and how you succeeded.

3. Share entries with the group (optional) and discuss strategies for improving self-control.
- Duration: 15-20 minutes daily

These expanded activities provide a variety of engaging and interactive ways for children to develop healthy coping skills, tolerance, and self-control. They encourage creativity, self-reflection, and practical application of these essential concepts.

Reflection:

- Journal: Write about a time when you used self-control to handle a situation.

Questions:

- What are some healthy ways to cope with stress?
- How can you practice tolerance in your daily life?
- When did you use self-control recently?

Week 7: Building Good Friendships and Managing Time

Objective: To develop good peer relationships, learn conflict resolution, address bullying, and improve time management.

Activities:

Peer Relationships

Friendship Bracelets

- Activity: Make friendship bracelets and give them to friends.

- Materials Needed: Embroidery floss or yarn, beads (optional), scissors.
- Instructions:
    1. Choose colors of floss or yarn that you and your friend like.
    2. Braid or knot the floss to create a bracelet.
    3. Add beads if desired.
    4. Give the bracelet to a friend and explain why they are unique to you.
- Duration: 20-30 minutes

Compliment Circle

- Activity: Sit in a circle and compliment each person.
- Materials Needed: None.
- Instructions:
    1. Sit in a circle with the group.
    2. Take turns complimenting the person next to you.
    3. Continue until everyone has received and given a compliment.
    4. Discuss how giving and receiving compliments makes you feel.
- Duration: 15-20 minutes

Additional Peer Relationships Activities

Friendship Tree

- Activity: Create a tree with leaves representing different friends and their qualities.
- Materials Needed: Large paper, markers, cut-out paper leaves.
- Instructions:
    1. Draw a large tree on the paper.

2. Write the names of friends on the leaves and attach them to the tree.
  3. Write the positive qualities of each friend on their leaf.
  4. Share your friendship tree with the group.
- Duration: 25-30 minutes

Friendship Bingo

- Activity: Play a bingo game to learn more about your friends.
- Materials Needed: Bingo cards with friendship-related prompts, markers, or chips.
- Instructions:
  1. Create bingo cards with prompts like "Find someone who likes the same hobby as you" or "Find someone who has the same favorite color."
  2. Find friends who match the prompts, marking off the squares.
  3. The first to get five in a row shouts "Bingo!" and wins a small prize.
- Duration: 20-25 minutes

Conflict Resolution

Conflict Role Play

- Activity: Role-play different conflict scenarios and practice resolving them peacefully.
- Materials Needed: Scenario cards.
- Instructions:
  1. Create cards with conflict scenarios (e.g., "Two friends want to play with the same toy").
  2. Act out the scenarios in pairs or small groups and practice resolving them.

3. Discuss the strategies used and how they helped resolve the conflict.
- Duration: 30-35 minutes

Peace Table

- Activity: Create a "peace table" to resolve conflicts with friends.
- Materials Needed: A small table, chairs, peace-themed decorations (e.g., peace signs, calming colors), paper, and pens.
- Instructions:
  1. Please set up a small table and decorate it with peace-themed items.
  2. Explain that the peace table is a place to go when you need to resolve a conflict.
  3. Practice using the peace table with a partner by discussing a minor disagreement and finding a peaceful solution.
  4. Encourage using the peace table whenever conflicts arise.
- Duration: 20-25 minutes

Additional Conflict Resolution Activities

Conflict Resolution Wheel

- Activity: Create a wheel with different conflict resolution strategies.
- Materials Needed: Paper plates, markers, brads.
- Instructions:
  1. Divide a paper plate into sections and write different conflict resolution strategies in each section (e.g., "Take a deep breath," "Use 'I' statements").

2. Attach a spinner with a brad to the center of the plate.
3. Spin the wheel to choose a strategy when resolving a conflict.
4. Practice using the wheel in different scenarios.
- Duration: 25-30 minutes

Conflict Resolution Stories

- Activity: Write and share stories about resolving conflicts.
- Materials Needed: Paper, pens, markers.
- Instructions:
    1. Please write a short story about a conflict and how it was resolved peacefully.
    2. Illustrate the story with drawings.
    3. Share your story with the group and discuss the resolution strategies used.
- Duration: 30-35 minutes

Addressing Bullies

Superhero Stories

- Activity: Write a story where you are the superhero standing up to a bully.
- Materials Needed: Paper, pens, markers.
- Instructions:
    1. Write a story where you are the superhero who stands up to a bully.
    2. Include how you use your superhero powers to help others and stop bullying.
    3. Illustrate your story with drawings.
    4. Share your story with the group and discuss the importance of standing up to bullies.
- Duration: 30-35 minutes

Assertiveness Practice

- Activity: Practice saying "no" and standing up for yourself in different situations.
- Materials Needed: Scenario cards.
- Instructions:
    1. Create cards with different scenarios where you might need to say "no" or stand up for yourself (e.g., "A friend asks you to do something you don't want to do").
    2. In pairs, practice responding assertively to the scenarios.
    3. Discuss how it felt to be assertive and why it's essential.
- Duration: 20-25 minutes

Additional Addressing Bullies Activities

Bully-Free Zone Posters

- Activity: Create posters promoting a bully-free zone.
- Materials Needed: Poster board, markers, stickers.
- Instructions:
    1. Design posters with messages promoting kindness and a bully-free environment.
    2. Use bright colors and cheerful images.
    3. Display the posters around the classroom or school.
    4. Discuss how promoting a positive environment can help prevent bullying.
- Duration: 25-30 minutes

Bully Busters Club

- Activity: Form a club dedicated to preventing bullying and promoting kindness.

- Materials Needed: Club name ideas, meeting schedule, and activity ideas.
- Instructions:
    1. Create a club with a fun name focused on preventing bullying.
    2. Plan regular meetings to discuss ways to promote kindness and address bullying.
    3. Organize activities like kindness challenges, peer support groups, and awareness campaigns.
    4. Encourage participation and leadership from all members.
- Duration: Ongoing

Time Management

Daily Planner

- Activity: Create a fun daily planner to organize your tasks and activities.
- Materials Needed: Blank planner templates, colored markers, and stickers.
- Instructions:
    1. Design a daily planner with sections for different tasks and activities.
    2. Decorate the planner with colors and stickers to make it fun and engaging.
    3. Fill in the planner with your daily schedule, including school, homework, chores, and free time.
    4. Discuss the importance of planning and staying organized.
- Duration: 25-30 minutes

Time Management Game

- Activity: Play a game where you must manage your time to complete different tasks.
- Materials Needed: Task cards, timer, game board (optional).
- Instructions:
    1. Create cards with different tasks and the time needed to complete them (e.g., "Read for 10 minutes," "Do homework for 20 minutes").
    2. Use a timer to track the time spent on each task.
    3. Move around a game board or keep score based on task completion.
    4. Discuss strategies for managing time effectively.
- Duration: 30-35 minutes

Additional Time Management Activities

Time Management Jar

- Activity: Create a jar with time management tips.
- Materials Needed: Jar, slips of paper, pens.
- Instructions:
    1. Write time management tips on slips of paper (e.g., "Set a timer for tasks," "Take breaks").
    2. Place the slips in the jar.
    3. Draw a slip each day and practice the tip.
    4. Discuss how each tip helps manage time better.
- Duration: 15-20 minutes

Time Blocking

- Activity: Practice time blocking to organize your day.
- Materials Needed: Blank daily schedule templates and colored markers.
- Instructions:

1. Divide your day into blocks of time for different activities (e.g., school, homework, playtime).
2. Color-code each block to make it visually appealing.
3. Fill in the schedule with your daily tasks and activities.
4. Discuss how time blocking helps manage time and stay focused.

- Duration: 20-25 minutes

These expanded activities provide various engaging and interactive ways for children to develop peer relationships, resolve conflicts, address bullying, and manage their time effectively. They encourage creativity, self-reflection, and practical application of these essential concepts.

Reflection:

- Journal: Write about a time when you resolved a conflict with a friend.

Questions:

- What makes a good friend?
- How can you peacefully resolve conflicts?
- What can you do if you see someone being bullied?
- How can you manage your time better?

Week 8: Practicing Self-Care and Wellbeing

Objective: To emphasize the importance of self-care and provide positive steps for maintaining well-being.

Activities:

Self-Care Tips

Self-Care Bingo

- Activity: Play a game with self-care activities like reading, bathing, or playing outside.
- Materials Needed: Bingo cards with self-care activities, markers, or chips.
- Instructions:
    1. Create bingo cards with different self-care activities in each square (e.g., "Read a book," "Take a bath," "Play outside").
    2. Distribute the bingo cards and markers or chips.
    3. As you call out self-care activities, participants mark off the corresponding squares.
    4. The first to get five in a row shouts "Bingo!" and wins a small prize.
- Duration: 20-30 minutes

Relaxation Station

- Activity: Set up a relaxation station with comfy pillows, books, and calming activities.
- Materials Needed: Pillows, blankets, books, coloring supplies, calming music.
- Instructions:
    1. Create a cozy corner with pillows and blankets.
    2. Provide a selection of books, coloring supplies, and calming music.

3. Encourage kids to spend time in the relaxation station when they need a break.
4. Discuss the importance of taking time to relax and recharge.
- Duration: Ongoing

Additional Self-Care Tips Activities

Self-Care Jar

- Activity: Create a jar filled with self-care ideas.
- Materials Needed: Jar, slips of paper, pens, decorative materials.
- Instructions:
    1. Write different self-care activities on slips of paper (e.g., "Go for a walk," "Listen to music").
    2. Decorate the jar.
    3. When stressed, draw a slip from the jar and do the activity.
    4. Discuss how self-care activities can help manage stress.
- Duration: 15-20 minutes

Self-Care Calendar

- Activity: Create a monthly calendar with daily self-care activities.
- Materials Needed: Blank calendar templates, markers, and stickers.
- Instructions:
    1. Fill in each day of the calendar with a different self-care activity.
    2. Decorate the calendar with markers and stickers.
    3. Follow the calendar throughout the month, completing each activity.

4. Reflect on how regular self-care impacts well-being.
- Duration: 20-25 minutes

Positive Steps for Wellbeing

Gratitude Jar

- Activity: Create a gratitude jar with notes about things you're thankful for.
- Materials Needed: Jar, slips of paper, pens, decorative materials.
- Instructions:
    1. Decorate the jar.
    2. Write notes about things you're thankful for on slips of paper.
    3. Place the notes in the jar.
    4. Read the notes when you need a reminder of the good things in your life.
- Duration: 15-20 minutes

Wellbeing Poster

- Activity: Make a poster with positive steps to maintain your well-being.
- Materials Needed: Poster board, markers, magazines for cutouts, glue.
- Instructions:
    1. Brainstorm positive steps for maintaining well-being (e.g., "Exercise regularly," "Eat healthy foods").
    2. Write or draw these steps on the poster board.
    3. Add pictures and words cut out from magazines to illustrate each step.
    4. Display the poster in a prominent place as a daily reminder.

- Duration: 30-35 minutes

Additional Positive Steps for Wellbeing Activities

Wellbeing Wheel

- Activity: Create a wheel with different aspects of well-being.
- Materials Needed: Paper plates, markers, brads.
- Instructions:
    1. Divide a paper plate into sections and label each section with a different aspect of well-being (e.g., physical, emotional, social, spiritual).
    2. Write positive steps for each aspect in the corresponding section.
    3. Attach a spinner with a brad to the center of the plate.
    4. Spin the wheel daily to focus on a different aspect of well-being.
- Duration: 25-30 minutes

Wellbeing Journal

- Activity: Keep a journal to track positive steps for well-being.
- Materials Needed: Journals or notebooks, pens, markers.
- Instructions:
    1. Write daily entries about positive steps you took for your well-being.
    2. Reflect on how these steps made you feel.
    3. Decorate the journal with drawings and stickers.
    4. Share entries with the group (optional) and discuss the impact of well-being practices.
- Duration: 15-20 minutes daily

Final Self-Care Assessment

Self-Care Survey

- Activity: Fill out a fun survey to see how well you're taking care of yourself and set goals for improvement.
- Materials Needed: Printed surveys, pens.
- Instructions:
    1. Distribute the self-care surveys.
    2. Have participants fill out the surveys, answering questions about their self-care habits.
    3. Review the results and identify areas for improvement.
    4. Set specific self-care goals based on the survey results.
    5. Discuss the importance of regular self-assessment and goal-setting for self-care.
- Duration: 20-25 minutes

Additional Final Self-Care Assessment Activities

Self-Care Reflection

- Activity: Reflect on your self-care practices and write about your experiences.
- Materials Needed: Journals or notebooks, pens.
- Instructions:
    1. Write about your self-care practices over the past month.
    2. Reflect on what worked well and what could be improved.
    3. Set new self-care goals for the next month.
    4. Share reflections with the group (optional) and discuss strategies for improvement.
- Duration: 20-25 minutes

Self-Care Check-In

- Activity: Regularly check in with a partner about your self-care practices.
- Materials Needed: None.
- Instructions:
    1. Pair up with a partner.
    2. Schedule regular check-ins (e.g., weekly) to discuss your self-care practices.
    3. Share successes and challenges.
    4. Offer support and encouragement to each other.
    5. Adjust self-care goals as needed based on the check-ins.
- Duration: 10-15 minutes per check-in

These expanded activities provide various engaging and interactive ways for children to develop self-care habits, take positive steps for well-being, and assess their self-care practices. They encourage creativity, self-reflection, and practical application of these essential concepts.

Reflection:

- Journal: Write about your favorite self-care activities and how they help you.

Questions:

- What are some of your favorite self-care activities?
- How can you make sure to take care of yourself every day?
- What are you thankful for today?

Conclusion

By completing this fun and engaging course, you'll learn essential skills to help you handle stress, solve problems, and take care of yourself. These skills will help you feel more confident and ready to face any challenges that come your way. Remember, you are strong, capable, and constantly growing!

Life Purpose Course Manual for Parents, Guardians, and Trusted Adults

Course Overview

Welcome to the Life Purpose Course! This self-paced program is designed to help you support youth in discovering and fulfilling their life purpose. Through weekly modules, you will learn how to guide youth in understanding their strengths, developing resilience, and setting meaningful goals. The course covers the stages of change, love languages, growth mindset, gratitude practices, life storytelling, visualization, and goal-setting.

Course Objectives

By the end of this course, participants will be able to:

1. Understand and teach the stages of change and love languages.
2. Foster a growth mindset in youth.
3. Encourage gratitude and integrate gratitude exercises.
4. Guide youth in maintaining a gratitude journal and envisioning their future.
5. Help youth tell their life story and reflect on their past, present, and future.
6. Facilitate visualization exercises for their best possible self in various contexts.
7. Assist youth in exploring and setting short-term and long-term goals.
8. Support youth in creating and achieving SMART goals.

Age-Specific Life Purpose Skills Stories

1. Child (Ages 5-10)

Story Overview: Emma, an 8-year-old girl, faced the challenge of adjusting to a new school after her family moved to a different city.

Experiences: Emma struggled with making new friends and feeling confident in her new environment. She often felt lonely and anxious.

Overcoming Barriers: With the support of her parents and teachers, Emma learned to manage her anxiety through breathing exercises and positive affirmations. She joined a school club, which helped her make friends and build confidence.

Role of Parents/Guardians and Trusted Adults: Emma's parents played a crucial role by encouraging her to express her feelings, providing reassurance, and fostering new social connections. Her teacher also supported her by creating a welcoming classroom environment.

Skills, Questions, and Tasks for Each Week:

- Week 1: Stages of Change and Love Languages
  - Skill: Understanding change and expressing love.
  - Question: "How did you feel about changing schools?"
  - Task: Discuss her love language and how it helps her feel supported.
- Week 2: Growth Mindset
  - Skill: Developing a growth mindset.
  - Question: "What new things can you learn at your new school?"

- - Task: Set a small learning goal for the week.
- Week 3: Gratitude and Gratitude Exercises
  - Skill: Practicing gratitude.
  - Question: "What are you thankful for today?"
  - Task: Write down three things she is grateful for each day.
- Week 4: Gratitude Journal and Envisioning the Future
  - Skill: Maintaining gratitude and future visualization.
  - Question: "How can being thankful help you feel better about school?"
  - Task: Draw a picture of herself in the future at her new school.
- Week 5: Telling Your Life Story
  - Skill: Reflecting on past experiences.
  - Question: "What was your favorite memory from your old school?"
  - Task: Create a timeline of her school experiences.
- Week 6: Best Possible Self Visualization
  - Skill: Visualizing success.
  - Question: "What does your best day at school look like?"
  - Task: Describe her best possible day at school.
- Week 7: Self-Goal Explorations
  - Skill: Setting short-term goals.
  - Question: "What do you want to achieve this month?"
  - Task: Write a goal for the next month and plan how to achieve it.
- Week 8: Creating SMART Goals
  - Skill: Developing SMART goals.
  - Question: "How can you make your goal specific and achievable?"
  - Task: Create a SMART goal related to school and outline steps to achieve it.

2. Adolescent (Ages 11-13)

Story Overview: Liam, a 12-year-old boy, struggled with bullying at school and found it challenging to cope with the stress and self-esteem issues that resulted from it.

Experiences: Liam felt isolated and scared to go to school. His grades began to slip, and he became withdrawn.

Overcoming Barriers: With the help of a school counselor, Liam learned strategies to deal with bullying, such as seeking help from trusted adults and practicing assertiveness. He also joined a martial arts class to build confidence and resilience.

Role of Parents/Guardians and Trusted Adults: Liam's parents and school counselor provided support by addressing the bullying issue with school authorities and encouraging Liam to talk about his experiences. The martial arts instructor also served as a positive role model.

Skills, Questions, and Tasks for Each Week:

- Week 1: Stages of Change and Love Languages
    - Skill: Understanding change and expressing love.
    - Question: "How has your experience with bullying changed over time?"
    - Task: Discuss his love language and how it affects his relationships.
- Week 2: Growth Mindset
    - Skill: Developing a growth mindset.
    - Question: "How can thinking positively help you in difficult situations?"
    - Task: Set a personal growth goal for the week.
- Week 3: Gratitude and Gratitude Exercises
    - Skill: Practicing gratitude.

- o Question: "What are you grateful for today?"
- o Task: Keep a daily gratitude journal.
- Week 4: Gratitude Journal and Envisioning the Future
  - o Skill: Maintaining gratitude and future visualization.
  - o Question: "How can gratitude help you overcome challenges?"
  - o Task: Visualize a future where he feels confident and safe at school.
- Week 5: Telling Your Life Story
  - o Skill: Reflecting on past experiences.
  - o Question: "How have your experiences shaped who you are today?"
  - o Task: Write a story about overcoming bullying.
- Week 6: Best Possible Self Visualization
  - o Skill: Visualizing success.
  - o Question: "What does your best self look like in different areas of your life?"
  - o Task: Describe his best possible self in school, at home, and in the community.
- Week 7: Self-Goal Explorations
  - o Skill: Setting short-term goals.
  - o Question: "What do you want to achieve in the next three months?"
  - o Task: Identify and write down goals for the next three months.
- Week 8: Creating SMART Goals
  - o Skill: Developing SMART goals.
  - o Question: "How can you make your goals specific and measurable?"
  - o Task: Create at least three SMART goals and outline steps to achieve them.

3. Teen (Ages 14-18)

Story Overview: Sophia, a 16-year-old girl, faced the challenge of balancing academic pressures with her responsibilities at home, leading to high stress and burnout.

Experiences: Sophia felt overwhelmed by her schoolwork and family duties. She struggled with time management and experienced frequent stress.

Overcoming Barriers: Sophia learned stress management techniques such as time management, prioritizing tasks, and taking breaks. She also sought support from her teachers and joined a study group to manage her academic workload better.

Role of Parents/Guardians and Trusted Adults: Sophia's parents supported her by helping her set realistic goals and encouraging her to take breaks. Her teachers provided additional academic support and resources.

Skills, Questions, and Tasks for Each Week:

- Week 1: Stages of Change and Love Languages
  - Skill: Understanding change and expressing love.
  - Question: "How has your approach to managing stress changed over time?"
  - Task: Reflect on her love language and how it helps her feel supported.
- Week 2: Growth Mindset
  - Skill: Developing a growth mindset.
  - Question: "How can a growth mindset help you manage your responsibilities?"
  - Task: Set a growth mindset goal for the week.
- Week 3: Gratitude and Gratitude Exercises
  - Skill: Practicing gratitude.

- Question: "What are you grateful for today?"
- Task: Maintain a gratitude journal.
- Week 4: Gratitude Journal and Envisioning the Future
  - Skill: Maintaining gratitude and future visualization.
  - Question: "How can gratitude influence your future success?"
  - Task: Visualize her future self achieving her goals.
- Week 5: Telling Your Life Story
  - Skill: Reflecting on past experiences.
  - Question: "What past experiences have taught you important lessons?"
  - Task: Write about a significant experience and its impact on her life.
- Week 6: Best Possible Self Visualization
  - Skill: Visualizing success.
  - Question: "What does your best self look like in different areas of your life?"
  - Task: Describe her best possible self in school, at home, and in the community.
- Week 7: Self-Goal Explorations
  - Skill: Setting short-term goals.
  - Question: "What do you want to achieve in the next six months?"
  - Task: Identify and write down goals for the next six months.
- Week 8: Creating SMART Goals
  - Skill: Developing SMART goals.
  - Question: "How can you make your goals specific and measurable?"
  - Task: Create at least three SMART goals and outline steps to achieve them.

Weekly Modules

Week 1: The Stages of Change and Love Languages

Introduction: Welcome to Week 1! This week, we will explore the stages of change and the concept of love languages. Understanding the stages of change helps you support youth through different phases of personal growth. Recognizing love languages improves communication and relationships.

Content:

- Stages of Change: Precontemplation, Contemplation, Preparation, Action, Maintenance, and Relapse.
- Love Languages: Words of affirmation, acts of service, receiving gifts, quality time, and physical touch.

Activities:

- Discuss examples of change.
- Take a love language quiz.

Skills, Questions, and Tasks:

- Question: "Can you think of a time you experienced a big change? How did you feel?"
- Task: Reflect on your love language and how it affects your interactions with youth.

Week 2: Growth Mindset

Introduction: In Week 2, we will focus on fostering a growth mindset. A growth mindset encourages youth to view challenges as opportunities to learn and grow rather than as obstacles.

Content:

- Growth Mindset vs. Fixed Mindset: Understanding the difference and the benefits of a growth mindset.

Activities:

- Identify areas where youth can apply a growth mindset.
- Discuss real-life examples of a growth mindset.

Skills, Questions, and Tasks:

- Question: "How can changing your mindset about a challenge help you overcome it?"
- Task: Encourage youth to set a growth mindset goal for the week.

Week 3: Gratitude and Gratitude Exercises

Introduction: Welcome to Week 3! This week, we will focus on gratitude and gratitude exercises. Practicing gratitude can significantly enhance emotional well-being and foster a positive outlook.

Content:

- Gratitude Practices: Daily gratitude exercises, expressing gratitude verbally, and writing thank you notes.

Activities:

- Start a daily gratitude journal.
- Write a thank you letter to someone.

Skills, Questions, and Tasks:

- Question: "What are three things you are grateful for today?"
- Task: Write a thank you letter to someone who has positively impacted your life.

Week 4: Gratitude Journal and Envisioning the Future

Introduction: In Week 4, we will continue focusing on gratitude by maintaining a gratitude journal and envisioning the future. This practice helps youth appreciate the present while planning for their future.

Content:

- Gratitude Journal: Maintaining a daily record of things you are grateful for.
- Envisioning the Future: Imagining future scenarios where gratitude plays a role.

Activities:

- Continue writing in the gratitude journal.
- Discuss and visualize future goals and aspirations.

Skills, Questions, and Tasks:

- Question: "How can being grateful today influence your future?"
- Task: Visualize your future self and write about the role of gratitude in your life.

Week 5: Telling Your Life Story – Past, Present, and Future

Introduction: Welcome to Week 5! This week, we will explore the importance of storytelling and reflection. By telling their life story, youth can better understand their past, appreciate their present, and plan for their future.

Content:

- Life Story: Reflecting on past experiences, understanding the present, and envisioning the future.

Activities:

- Write or tell your life story, focusing on significant past experiences, current goals, and future aspirations.

Skills, Questions, and Tasks:

- Question: "What experiences from your past have shaped who you are today?"

- Task: Create a timeline of significant life events and discuss how they have impacted you.

Week 6: Best Possible Self Visualization Exercise – In School, With Family, and In the Community

Introduction: In Week 6, we will practice a visualization exercise to imagine the best possible version of yourself in different contexts. This exercise helps youth set aspirational goals and see themselves achieving their best.

Content:

- Best Possible Self: Visualizing success and positive outcomes in school, with family, and in the community.

Activities:

- Conduct a visualization exercise imagining your best self in different areas of life.

Skills, Questions, and Tasks:

- Question: "What does your best self look like at school, with family, and in the community?"
- Task: Write a detailed description of your best self in each context.

Week 7: Self-Goal Explorations – One Month, Three Months, and Six Months

Introduction: Welcome to Week 7! This week, we will explore goal setting by identifying goals for the next month, three months, and six months. Setting short-term and long-term goals helps youth stay focused and motivated.

Content:

- Goal Setting: Identifying and setting realistic and achievable goals.

Activities:

- Identify goals for the next month, three months, and six months.
- Create a plan to achieve these goals.

Skills, Questions, and Tasks:

- Question: "What is one goal you want to achieve in the next month? Three months? Six months?"
- Task: Write down your goals and create a step-by-step plan.

Week 8: Create Your Final SMART Goals

Introduction: In the final week, we will focus on creating SMART goals (Specific, Measurable, Achievable, Relevant, and Time-bound). SMART goals provide a clear roadmap for achieving your objectives.

Content:

- SMART Goals: Understanding and applying the SMART criteria to goal setting.

Activities:

- Review your previous goals and refine them into SMART goals.
- Develop an action plan to achieve your SMART goals.

Skills, Questions, and Tasks:

- Question: "How can you make your goals more specific and measurable?"
- Task: Create at least three SMART goals and outline the steps to achieve them.

Overall Conclusion

This Life Purpose Course will equip you with the tools and knowledge to help youth discover and fulfill their life purpose. You can guide youth in building resilience, understanding their strengths, and achieving their goals. Remember, each youth's journey is unique, and with the proper support and strategies, they can thrive and succeed in their endeavors.

Life Purpose Course for Youth

Course Overview

Welcome to the Life Purpose Course! This course will help you discover your unique life purpose and develop your skills to achieve your goals. Each week, we will explore different topics and activities that will guide you in understanding yourself better, setting goals, and creating a plan for your future.

Course Objectives

By the end of this course, you will be able to:

1. Understand the stages of change and how they apply to your life.
2. Recognize your love language and how it affects your relationships.
3. Develop a growth mindset and learn to see challenges as opportunities.
4. Practice gratitude and understand its impact on your well-being.
5. Reflect on your life story and appreciate your past, present, and future.
6. Visualize your best possible self in different areas of your life.
7. Explore and set short-term and long-term goals.
8. Create and achieve SMART goals.

Age-Specific Life Purpose Skills Stories

1. Child (Ages 5-10)

Story Overview: Emma, an 8-year-old girl, faced the challenge of adjusting to a new school after her family moved to a different city.

Experiences: Emma struggled with making new friends and feeling confident in her new environment. She often felt lonely and anxious.

Overcoming Barriers: With the support of her parents and teachers, Emma learned to manage her anxiety through breathing exercises and positive affirmations. She joined a school club, which helped her make friends and build confidence.

Role of Parents/Guardians and Trusted Adults: Emma's parents played a crucial role by encouraging her to express her feelings, providing reassurance, and fostering new social connections. Her teacher also supported her by creating a welcoming classroom environment.

Skills, Questions, and Tasks for Each Week:

- Week 1: Stages of Change and Love Languages
  - Skill: Understanding change and expressing love.
  - Question: "How did you feel about changing schools?"
  - Task: Discuss her love language and how it helps her feel supported.
- Week 2: Growth Mindset
  - Skill: Developing a growth mindset.
  - Question: "What new things can you learn at your new school?"

- - Task: Set a small learning goal for the week.
- Week 3: Gratitude and Gratitude Exercises
  - Skill: Practicing gratitude.
  - Question: "What are you thankful for today?"
  - Task: Write down three things she is grateful for each day.
- Week 4: Gratitude Journal and Envisioning the Future
  - Skill: Maintaining gratitude and future visualization.
  - Question: "How can being thankful help you feel better about school?"
  - Task: Draw a picture of herself in the future at her new school.
- Week 5: Telling Your Life Story
  - Skill: Reflecting on past experiences.
  - Question: "What was your favorite memory from your old school?"
  - Task: Create a timeline of her school experiences.
- Week 6: Best Possible Self Visualization
  - Skill: Visualizing success.
  - Question: "What does your best day at school look like?"
  - Task: Describe her best possible day at school.
- Week 7: Self-Goal Explorations
  - Skill: Setting short-term goals.
  - Question: "What do you want to achieve this month?"
  - Task: Write a goal for the next month and plan how to achieve it.
- Week 8: Creating SMART Goals
  - Skill: Developing SMART goals.
  - Question: "How can you make your goal specific and achievable?"
  - Task: Create a SMART goal related to school and outline steps to achieve it.

2. Adolescent (Ages 11-13)

Story Overview: Liam, a 12-year-old boy, struggled with bullying at school and found it challenging to cope with the stress and self-esteem issues that resulted from it.

Experiences: Liam felt isolated and scared to go to school. His grades began to slip, and he became withdrawn.

Overcoming Barriers: With the help of a school counselor, Liam learned strategies to deal with bullying, such as seeking help from trusted adults and practicing assertiveness. He also joined a martial arts class to build confidence and resilience.

Role of Parents/Guardians and Trusted Adults: Liam's parents and school counselor provided support by addressing the bullying issue with school authorities and encouraging Liam to talk about his experiences. The martial arts instructor also served as a positive role model.

Skills, Questions, and Tasks for Each Week:

- Week 1: Stages of Change and Love Languages
    - Skill: Understanding change and expressing love.
    - Question: "How has your experience with bullying changed over time?"
    - Task: Discuss his love language and how it affects his relationships.
- Week 2: Growth Mindset
    - Skill: Developing a growth mindset.
    - Question: "How can thinking positively help you in difficult situations?"
    - Task: Set a personal growth goal for the week.
- Week 3: Gratitude and Gratitude Exercises
    - Skill: Practicing gratitude.

- o Question: "What are you grateful for today?"
- o Task: Keep a daily gratitude journal.
- Week 4: Gratitude Journal and Envisioning the Future
  - o Skill: Maintaining gratitude and future visualization.
  - o Question: "How can gratitude help you overcome challenges?"
  - o Task: Visualize a future where he feels confident and safe at school.
- Week 5: Telling Your Life Story
  - o Skill: Reflecting on past experiences.
  - o Question: "How have your experiences shaped who you are today?"
  - o Task: Write a story about overcoming bullying.
- Week 6: Best Possible Self Visualization
  - o Skill: Visualizing success.
  - o Question: "What does your best self look like in different areas of your life?"
  - o Task: Describe his best possible self in school, at home, and in the community.
- Week 7: Self-Goal Explorations
  - o Skill: Setting short-term goals.
  - o Question: "What do you want to achieve in the next three months?"
  - o Task: Identify and write down goals for the next three months.
- Week 8: Creating SMART Goals
  - o Skill: Developing SMART goals.
  - o Question: "How can you make your goals specific and measurable?"
  - o Task: Create at least three SMART goals and outline steps to achieve them.

3. Teen (Ages 14-18)

Story Overview: Sophia, a 16-year-old girl, faced the challenge of balancing academic pressures with her responsibilities at home, leading to high stress and burnout.

Experiences: Sophia felt overwhelmed by her schoolwork and family duties. She struggled with time management and experienced frequent stress.

Overcoming Barriers: Sophia learned stress management techniques such as time management, prioritizing tasks, and taking breaks. She also sought support from her teachers and joined a study group to manage her academic workload better.

Role of Parents/Guardians and Trusted Adults: Sophia's parents supported her by helping her set realistic goals and encouraging her to take breaks. Her teachers provided additional academic support and resources.

Skills, Questions, and Tasks for Each Week:

- Week 1: Stages of Change and Love Languages
    - Skill: Understanding change and expressing love.
    - Question: "How has your approach to managing stress changed over time?"
    - Task: Reflect on her love language and how it helps her feel supported.
- Week 2: Growth Mindset
    - Skill: Developing a growth mindset.
    - Question: "How can a growth mindset help you manage your responsibilities?"
    - Task: Set a growth mindset goal for the week.
- Week 3: Gratitude and Gratitude Exercises
    - Skill: Practicing gratitude.

- o Question: "What are you grateful for today?"
- o Task: Maintain a gratitude journal.
- Week 4: Gratitude Journal and Envisioning the Future
  - o Skill: Maintaining gratitude and future visualization.
  - o Question: "How can gratitude influence your future success?"
  - o Task: Visualize her future self achieving her goals.
- Week 5: Telling Your Life Story
  - o Skill: Reflecting on past experiences.
  - o Question: "What past experiences have taught you important lessons?"
  - o Task: Write about a significant experience and its impact on her life.
- Week 6: Best Possible Self Visualization
  - o Skill: Visualizing success.
  - o Question: "What does your best self look like in different areas of your life?"
  - o Task: Describe her best possible self in school, at home, and in the community.
- Week 7: Self-Goal Explorations
  - o Skill: Setting short-term goals.
  - o Question: "What do you want to achieve in the next six months?"
  - o Task: Identify and write down goals for the next six months.
- Week 8: Creating SMART Goals
  - o Skill: Developing SMART goals.
  - o Question: "How can you make your goals specific and measurable?"
  - o Task: Create at least three SMART goals and outline steps to achieve them.

Weekly Modules

Week 1: The Stages of Change and Love Languages

Introduction: Welcome to Week 1! This week, we will learn about the stages of change and the concept of love languages. Understanding these will help you navigate personal growth and improve your relationships with others.

Content:

Stages of Change:

1. Precontemplation: In this stage, individuals are unaware of the need for change or are unwilling to change. They may not see their behavior as problematic.
2. Contemplation: Here, people recognize the need for change and are considering taking action but have yet to commit to it.
3. Preparation: At this point, individuals are ready to take action and may make small steps towards change.
4. Action: This is where active, observable changes in behavior occur. People are modifying their habits and environment to support the change.
5. Maintenance: In this stage, people work to sustain their changes and prevent relapse.
6. Relapse: This can occur at any point in the process. It involves returning to old behaviors, but it's considered a normal part of the change process.

Love Languages:

1. Words of Affirmation: People with this love language value verbal expressions of love, praise, and appreciation.
2. Acts of Service: These individuals feel loved when others do things to help them or make their lives easier.
3. Receiving Gifts: For these people, thoughtful presents and tokens of affection are significant.
4. Quality Time: Those with this love language value undivided attention and shared experiences.
5. Physical Touch: People with this love language feel loved through physical affection like hugs, hand-holding, or comforting touches.

Understanding these concepts can help in personal growth, relationship building, and supporting others through change processes.

Activities:

- Discuss examples of change you've experienced.
- Take a love language quiz to discover your love language.

Questions and Tasks:

- Question: "Can you think of a time you experienced a big change? How did you feel?"
- Task: Reflect on your love language and how it helps you feel supported.

Week 2: Growth Mindset

Introduction: In Week 2, we will focus on developing a growth mindset. A growth mindset helps you view challenges as opportunities to learn and grow.

Content:

Growth Mindset:

1. Definition: Belief that abilities and intelligence can be developed through effort, learning, and persistence.
2. Characteristics:
    - Embraces challenges
    - Persists in the face of setbacks
    - Sees effort as a path to mastery
    - Learns from criticism
    - Finds inspiration in others' success
3. Outcomes:
    - Higher achievement
    - Increased resilience
    - Greater willingness to take on challenges

Fixed Mindset:

1. Definition: Belief that essential qualities, like intelligence or talent, are fixed traits.
2. Characteristics:
    - Avoids challenges
    - Gives up easily
    - Sees effort as fruitless
    - Ignores useful feedback
    - Feels threatened by others' success
3. Outcomes:
    - Lower achievement potential
    - Decreased resilience

- Tendency to avoid challenges

Benefits of a Growth Mindset:

1. Improved learning and academic performance
2. Increased resilience and ability to overcome obstacles
3. Enhanced problem-solving skills
4. Greater self-awareness and self-esteem
5. Improved relationships and collaboration skills
6. Increased motivation and productivity
7. Better ability to handle change and adapt to new situations

Understanding these mindsets' differences can help individuals, especially children and young adults, approach learning and challenges more positively. By fostering a growth mindset, parents and educators can help children develop resilience, embrace challenges, and achieve their full potential.

Activities:

- Identify areas where you can apply a growth mindset.
- Discuss real-life examples of a growth mindset.

Questions and Tasks:

- Question: "How can changing your mindset about a challenge help you overcome it?"
- Task: Set a growth mindset goal for the week.

Week 3: Gratitude and Gratitude Exercises

Introduction: Welcome to Week 3! This week, we will focus on practicing gratitude. Gratitude can significantly enhance your emotional well-being and foster a positive outlook.

Content:

1. Daily Gratitude Exercises:
   - Set aside time each day to reflect on things you're grateful for
   - Keep a gratitude journal, writing down 3-5 things daily
   - Use gratitude prompts or apps to inspire reflection
   - Practice mindful appreciation of everyday experiences
   - Start or end your day with a gratitude meditation
2. Expressing Gratitude Verbally:
   - Make a conscious effort to thank people in your daily interactions
   - Share your appreciation for others during conversations
   - Acknowledge specific actions or qualities you're grateful for in others
   - Practice expressing gratitude in various settings (home, work, social)
   - Use phone calls or video chats to express gratitude to distant loved ones
3. Writing Thank You Notes:
   - Set a goal to write a certain number of thank you notes per week or month
   - Keep a stack of cards or stationary ready for impromptu notes
   - Write detailed, specific notes explaining why you're grateful
   - Send thank you emails or messages for more minor gestures
   - Consider writing notes to people from your past who've positively impacted you

By incorporating these practices, individuals can cultivate a more grateful mindset, improve relationships, and enhance overall well-being. These exercises can be particularly beneficial for children, helping them develop emotional intelligence and appreciation for others from a young age.

Activities:

- Start a daily gratitude journal.
- Write a thank you letter to someone who has helped you.

Questions and Tasks:

- Question: "What are three things you are grateful for today?"
- Task: Write a thank you letter to someone who has positively impacted your life.

Week 4: Gratitude Journal and Envisioning the Future

Introduction: In Week 4, we will continue focusing on gratitude by maintaining a gratitude journal and envisioning your future. This practice helps you appreciate the present while planning for your future.

Content:

1. Gratitude Journal:

    Definition: A daily record of things you are grateful for.

    Key components:

    - Consistency: Writing entries daily or regularly

- Specificity: Noting particular things, people, or experiences
- Reflection: Thinking deeply about why you're grateful

Steps to maintain:
a. Choose a journal or digital app
b. Set a specific time each day for journaling
c. Write 3-5 things you're grateful for
d. Be specific and detailed in your entries
e. Reflect on how these things positively impact your life
benefits:

- Increases awareness of positive aspects of life
- Improves mood and overall well-being
- Enhances perspective during challenging times

2. Envisioning the Future with Gratitude:

Definition: Imagining future scenarios where gratitude plays a significant role.

Key components:

- Visualization: Creating mental images of future events
- Positive focus: Emphasizing gratitude in these scenarios
- Goal-setting: Using gratitude as a motivator for future aspirations

Steps to practice:
a. Set aside time for quiet reflection
b. Imagine specific future events or achievements
c. Visualize feeling grateful in these scenarios
d. Consider how gratitude might influence your actions

and decisions
e. Use these visions to set positive goals and benefits:

- Cultivates a positive outlook on the future
- Motivates goal-directed behavior
- Enhances resilience and optimism

Both practices aim to foster a more grateful mindset, which can lead to increased happiness, improved relationships, and better mental health.

Activities:

- Continue writing in your gratitude journal.
- Discuss and visualize your future goals and aspirations.

Questions and Tasks:

- Question: "How can being grateful today influence your future?"
- Task: Visualize your future self and write about the role of gratitude in your life.

Week 5: Telling Your Life Story – Past, Present, and Future

Introduction: Welcome to Week 5! This week, we will explore the importance of storytelling and reflection. By telling your life story, you can better understand your past, appreciate your present, and plan for your future.

Content:

1. Reflecting on Past Experiences:
    - Definition: Looking back at significant events, decisions, and moments.
    - Purpose: To understand how past experiences have shaped who you are today.
    - Activities:
        - I am journaling about crucial life events and their impact.
        - We were discussing past experiences with a trusted friend or mentor.
        - We are creating a timeline of significant life moments.
2. Understanding the Present:
    - Definition: Analyzing your current situation, feelings, and behaviors.
    - Purpose: To gain insight into your current state of mind and circumstances.
    - Activities:
        - You are assessing your current emotional, physical, and spiritual well-being.
        - We are identifying current challenges and strengths.
        - I practice mindfulness to stay present and aware of my thoughts and feelings.
3. Envisioning the Future:
    - Definition: Imagining future scenarios and setting goals for your goals.
    - Purpose: Create a vision for your future incorporating gratitude and positive aspirations.
    - Activities:
        - I am setting SMART goals for personal and professional growth.

- Visualizing future successes and the role gratitude will play in them.
- I am creating a vision board to represent your future aspirations.

By reflecting on the past, understanding the present, and envisioning the future, individuals can understand their life story comprehensively, which can help in personal growth and resilience.

Activities:

- Write or tell your life story, focusing on significant past experiences, current goals, and future aspirations.

Questions and Tasks:

- Question: "What experiences from your past have shaped who you are today?"
- Task: Create a timeline of significant life events and discuss how they have impacted you.

Week 6: Best Possible Self Visualization Exercise – In School, With Family, and In the Community

Introduction: In Week 6, we will practice a visualization exercise to imagine the best possible version of yourself in different contexts. This exercise helps you set aspirational goals and see yourself achieving your best.

Content:

Best Possible Self: An Overview

The Best Possible Self (BPS) exercise is a positive psychology intervention that involves visualizing and writing about your ideal future self. This technique aims to boost optimism, improve mood, and increase motivation for personal growth.

Key Components

1. Visualization

> You are mentally picturing yourself in various optimistic scenarios, achieving your goals, and living your best life.

2. Positive Outcomes

> Focusing on successful results and favorable situations rather than obstacles or failures.

3. Multiple Life Domains

> Applying this technique to different areas of your life for a well-rounded approach.

Application in Different Areas

In School

- Visualizing academic success (e.g., high grades, understanding complex concepts)
- Imagining positive relationships with teachers and peers

- Picturing yourself confidently presenting or participating in class discussions
- Envisioning future educational achievements (e.g., graduation, scholarships)

With Family

- Imagining harmonious relationships with family members
- Visualizing supportive and open communication within the family
- Picturing shared positive experiences and quality time
- Envisioning your role in contributing to family well-being

In the Community

- Visualizing yourself as an active and valued community member
- Imagining successful participation in community projects or events
- Picturing positive interactions with neighbors and local organizations
- Envisioning the positive impact you could have on your community

Benefits of the Best Possible Self-Exercise

- Increases optimism and positive emotions
- Enhances motivation and goal-setting abilities
- Improves overall well-being and life satisfaction
- It helps in developing a clearer vision for personal growth and success

By regularly practicing this visualization technique across these different life domains, individuals can cultivate a more positive outlook and work towards achieving their full potential in various aspects of their lives.

Activities:

- Conduct a visualization exercise imagining your best self in different areas of life.

Questions and Tasks:

- Question: "What does your best self look like at school, with family, and in the community?"
- Task: Describe your best possible self in each context.

Week 7: Self-Goal Explorations – One Month, Three Months, and Six Months

Introduction: Welcome to Week 7! This week, we will explore goal setting by identifying goals for the next month, three months, and six months. Setting short-term and long-term goals helps you stay focused and motivated.

Content:

Components of Effective Goal Setting

1. Identifying Goals

- Reflect on personal aspirations and ambitions
- Consider areas for improvement or growth
- Align goals with long-term vision and values
- Prioritize goals based on importance and urgency

2. Setting Realistic Goals

- Ensure goals are attainable given current resources and circumstances
- Break larger goals into smaller, manageable steps
- Consider potential obstacles and plan for them
- Set goals that challenge you but are within reach

3. Making Goals Achievable

- Use the SMART criteria to refine goals:
    - Specific: Clearly define what you want to accomplish
    - Measurable: Establish concrete criteria for measuring progress
    - Achievable: Ensure the goal is realistic given your resources and constraints
    - Relevant: Align the goal with your broader objectives
    - Time-bound: Set a clear deadline or timeframe

Strategies for Effective Goal Setting

1. Write down your goals to increase commitment and clarity
2. Break larger goals into smaller, actionable steps
3. Set both short-term and long-term goals to maintain motivation
4. Regularly review and adjust goals as needed
5. Visualize success to boost motivation and focus
6. Create a supportive environment by sharing goals with others
7. Celebrate milestones and small victories along the way

Benefits of Proper Goal Setting

- Provides direction and focus
- Increases motivation and commitment
- Improves time management and productivity
- Enhances self-confidence as goals are achieved
- Facilitates personal and professional growth

By following these strategies and principles, you can set realistic and achievable goals, increasing your chances of success and personal development.

Activities:

- Identify goals for the next month, three months, and six months.
- Create a plan to achieve these goals.

Questions and Tasks:

- Question: "What is one goal you want to achieve in the next month? Three months? Six months?"
- Task: Write down your goals and create a step-by-step plan.

Week 8: Create Your Final SMART Goals

Introduction: In the final week, we will focus on creating SMART goals (Specific, Measurable, Achievable, Relevant, and Time-bound). SMART goals provide a clear roadmap for achieving your objectives.

Content:

- SMART Goals: Understanding and applying the SMART criteria to goal setting.

The SMART criteria is a widely used framework for setting practical goals. Let's break down each component of SMART goals and how to apply them:

S: Specific

A specific goal clearly defines what needs to be accomplished, who is responsible, and what steps are required.

- Ask questions like: What exactly do I want to achieve? Who is involved? What resources are needed?
- Example: Instead of "I want to get in shape," a specific goal would be "I want to obtain a gym membership and work out four days a week to be healthier."

M: Measurable

Measurable goals have criteria for tracking progress and determining when the goal has been achieved.

- Ask: How much? How many? How will I know when it's accomplished?
- Example: "I will aim to lose one pound of body fat weekly."

A: Achievable

Given your current resources and constraints, an achievable goal is realistic and attainable.

- Consider: Do I have the necessary skills and resources? Are there any limitations or constraints?
- The goal should be challenging but possible to accomplish.

R: Relevant

A relevant goal aligns with your broader objectives and long-term vision.

- Ask: Does this goal align with my other goals? Is it worthwhile? Is this the right time?
- Ensure the goal fits with your overall plans and values.

T: Time-bound

Time-bound goals have a clear start and end date, creating a sense of urgency and motivation.

- Specify: When will I start? When is the deadline? What can I do today?
- Example: "By the end of August, I will have achieved my goal if I lose four pounds of fat over the month."

Applying SMART Criteria

1. Write down your goal using the SMART framework.
2. Use action verbs to make objectives clear and specific.
3. Include measurable benchmarks for tracking progress.
4. Ensure the goal is realistic, given your current situation.
5. Align the goal with your broader objectives and values.
6. Set a clear timeline with specific start and end dates.

By applying these SMART criteria, you can create well-defined, achievable goals that provide clear direction and increase your chances of success. Remember to review and adjust your goals to stay on track regularly.

Activities:

- Review your previous goals and refine them into SMART goals.
- Develop an action plan to achieve your SMART goals.

Questions and Tasks:

- Question: "How can you make your goals more specific and measurable?"
- Task: Create at least three SMART goals and outline the steps to achieve them.

Overall Conclusion

Congratulations on completing the Life Purpose Course! You now have the tools to understand yourself better, set meaningful goals, and create a plan to achieve them. Remember, discovering your life purpose is a journey; taking it one step at a time is okay. Keep practicing the skills you've learned, stay resilient, and continue to seek support from your parents, guardians, and trusted adults. Your unique path is unfolding, and you have the power to shape your future with confidence and purpose. Good luck!

Empowerment Course Manual

Course Overview

Welcome to the Empowerment Course, designed for parents, guardians, and trusted adults to learn how to support youth in developing resilience and coping skills. This self-paced course will cover various aspects of empowerment, including stress management, success, gratitude, self-esteem, protective factors, stages of change, social supports, values, strengths, and problem-solving. By understanding and implementing these elements, you will be equipped to help youth navigate challenges and thrive.

Course Objectives

By the end of this course, participants will be able to:

1. Understand and apply the stages of change to support youth in their development.
2. Identify and enhance protective factors and social supports for youth.
3. Cultivate gratitude through exercises and journaling.
4. Foster self-esteem by exploring values, strengths, and positive qualities.
5. Promote stress management techniques and awareness.
6. Guide youth in effective problem-solving strategies.
7. Encourage self-care and healthy choices for overall well-being.

Weekly Introductions

Week 1: The Stages of Change and a Self-Care Assessment

Introduction: Welcome to Week 1. This week, we will explore the stages of change and conduct a self-care assessment. Understanding the stages of change will help you support youth through different phases of personal growth. The self-care evaluation will provide a baseline to identify areas that need attention.

Week 2: Protective Factors and Social Supports

Introduction: In Week 2, we will focus on identifying protective factors and building social support. These elements are crucial in fostering resilience and providing a safety net for youth as they navigate life's challenges.

Week 3: Love Languages, Gratitude Exercises, Gratitude Journal & Thank You Letter

Introduction: Welcome to Week 3. This week, we will explore the concept of love languages and the practice of gratitude. Engaging in gratitude exercises, maintaining a gratitude journal, and writing thank you letters can significantly boost emotional well-being and strengthen relationships.

Week 4: Values Exploration, My Strengths/Qualities & Self-Esteem

Introduction: In Week 4, we will delve into values exploration, identifying strengths and qualities, and building self-esteem. Understanding personal values and recognizing strengths are critical to developing a solid self-worth.

Week 5: Life Exploration, Positive Experiences

Introduction: Welcome to Week 5. This week, we will encourage life exploration and reflection on positive experiences. Recognizing and building on positive experiences can foster a sense of achievement and motivation.

Week 6: Stress Awareness & Stress Management

Introduction: In Week 6, we will focus on stress awareness and management techniques. Understanding the sources and signs of stress and learning effective coping strategies will help youth maintain emotional balance.

Week 7: Problem Solving

Introduction: Welcome to Week 7. This week, we will explore problem-solving skills. Practical problem-solving abilities are essential for navigating challenges and making informed decisions.

Week 8: Self-Care Tips, Positive Steps for Wellbeing, Healthy Choices, and Final Self-Care Assessment

Introduction: In the final week, we will review self-care tips, positive steps for well-being, and healthy choices. We will also conduct a final self-care assessment to evaluate progress and identify areas for continued growth.

Age-Specific Resilience and Coping Skills Stories

1. Child (Ages 5-10)

Story Overview: Emma, an 8-year-old girl, faced the challenge of adjusting to a new school after her family moved to a different city.

Experiences: Emma struggled with making new friends and feeling confident in her new environment. She often felt lonely and anxious.

Overcoming Barriers: With the support of her parents and teachers, Emma learned to manage her anxiety through breathing exercises and positive affirmations. She joined a school club, which helped her make friends and build confidence.

Role of Parents/Guardians and Trusted Adults: Emma's parents played a crucial role by encouraging her to express her feelings, providing reassurance, and fostering new social connections. Her teacher also supported her by creating a welcoming classroom environment.

Skills, Questions, and Tasks:

- Stress Management: Teach Emma breathing exercises. Question: "How do you feel after doing the breathing exercise?"
- Success: Celebrate small achievements. Task: Create a "Success Jar" where Emma can drop notes of her daily successes.
- Gratitude: Start a gratitude journal. Task: Write three things Emma is grateful for each day.
- Self-Esteem: Identify strengths. Question: "What do you like most about yourself?"

- Protective Factors: Encourage participation in group activities. Task: Join a club or team.
- Stages of Change: Discuss feelings about the new school. Question: "How do you feel about your new school now compared to when you first started?"
- Social Supports: Help her make friends. Task: Plan a playdate with a classmate.
- Values: Discuss what is important to her. Question: "What do you think is the most important quality in a friend?"
- Strengths: Identify and praise her strengths. Task: Draw a picture of herself doing something she's good at.
- Problem Solving: Role-play social scenarios. Task: Practice what to say when meeting a new friend.

2. Adolescent (Ages 11-13)

Story Overview: Liam, a 12-year-old boy, faced bullying at school, which affected his self-esteem and academic performance.

Experiences: Liam felt isolated and stressed due to the bullying. He struggled with speaking up and seeking help.

Overcoming Barriers: Liam's parents and school counselor worked together to address the bullying. Liam participated in a peer support group where he learned assertiveness and coping skills.

Role of Parents/Guardians and Trusted Adults: Liam's parents provided a safe and supportive home environment, regularly checked in on his feelings, and communicated with school officials to ensure the bullying was addressed.

Skills, Questions, and Tasks:

- Stress Management: Teach relaxation techniques. Question: "What relaxation technique helps you the most?"
- Success: Set academic and personal goals. Task: Create a goal chart.
- Gratitude: Write thank you notes. Task: Write a thank you note to someone who has helped him.
- Self-Esteem: Build positive self-talk. Question: "What positive things can you say to yourself daily?"
- Protective Factors: Foster connections with positive peers. Task: Identify and spend time with supportive friends.
- Stages of Change: Discuss his feelings about the bullying situation. Question: "How have your feelings changed since the bullying started?"
- Social Supports: Encourage participation in supportive groups. Task: Join a peer support group or club.
- Values: Reflect on personal values. Question: "What values are most important when choosing friends?"
- Strengths: Identify and focus on his strengths. Task: Write a list of personal strengths and achievements.
- Problem Solving: Develop a plan for dealing with bullying. Task: Create a step-by-step plan for handling bullying situations.

3. Teen (Ages 14-18)

Story Overview: Sophia, a 16-year-old girl, struggled to balance academic pressures with extracurricular activities and a part-time job.

Experiences: Sophia experienced high stress levels and burnout, impacting her health and academic performance.

Overcoming Barriers: Sophia learned time management and stress reduction techniques. She prioritized her activities and practiced mindfulness to manage her stress.

Role of Parents/Guardians and Trusted Adults: Sophia's parents supported her by helping her reorganize her schedule, encouraging her to take breaks, and promoting a balanced lifestyle.

Skills, Questions, and Tasks:

- Stress Management: Practice mindfulness. Task: Engage in daily mindfulness exercises.
- Success: Celebrate achievements. Question: "What are some recent successes you're proud of?"
- Gratitude: Maintain a gratitude journal. Task: Write daily entries about things for which she is grateful.
- Self-Esteem: Encourage positive affirmations. Task: Write and repeat daily affirmations.
- Protective Factors: Maintain a balanced schedule. Task: Create a balanced weekly schedule.
- Stages of Change: Reflect on stress levels. Question: "How do you feel about your current stress levels compared to before?"
- Social Supports: Build a support network. Task: Identify and connect with supportive friends and mentors.
- Values: Explore personal values. Question: "What values guide your decisions and actions?"
- Strengths: Focus on strengths. Task: List strengths and how they can be applied to daily challenges.
- Problem Solving: Develop problem-solving skills. Task: Work through a current problem using a step-by-step approach.

Program Schedule

Week 1: The Stages of Change and a Self-Care Assessment

Introduction: This week, we will explore the stages of change and conduct a self-care assessment. Understanding the stages of change will help you support youth through different phases of personal growth. The self-care evaluation will provide a baseline to identify areas that need attention.

Skills, Questions, and Tasks:

- Stages of Change: Discuss examples of change. Question: "Can you think of a time you experienced a big change?"
- Self-Care Assessment: Conduct a self-care assessment. Task: Complete the self-care assessment form.

Week 2: Protective Factors and Social Supports

Introduction: We will focus on identifying protective factors and building social support. These elements are crucial in fostering resilience and providing a safety net for youth as they navigate life's challenges.

Skills, Questions, and Tasks:

- Protective Factors: Identify protective factors in youth's lives. Task: List five protective factors.
- Social Supports: Map out social support networks. Question: "Who can you turn to for support?"

Week 3: Love Languages, Gratitude Exercises, Gratitude Journal & Thank You Letter

Introduction: This week, we will explore the concept of love languages and the practice of gratitude. Engaging in gratitude exercises, maintaining a gratitude journal, and writing thank you letters can significantly boost emotional well-being and strengthen relationships.

Skills, Questions, and Tasks:

- Love Languages: Identify personal love languages. Task: Take a love language quiz.
- Gratitude Exercises: Practice daily gratitude. Task: Start a gratitude journal and write daily entries.
- Thank You Letter: Write a thank you letter. Task: Write and send a thank you letter to someone special.

Week 4: Values Exploration, My Strengths/Qualities & Self-Esteem

Introduction: We will explore values exploration, identifying strengths and qualities, and building self-esteem. Understanding personal values and recognizing strengths are critical to developing a solid self-worth.

Skills, Questions, and Tasks:

- Values Exploration: Reflect on values. Question: "What values are most important to you?"
- Strengths/Qualities: Identify strengths. Task: List ten personal strengths or qualities.
- Self-Esteem: Build self-esteem through affirmations. Task: Create and repeat positive affirmations daily.

Week 5: Life Exploration, Positive Experiences

Introduction: This week, we will encourage life exploration and reflection on positive experiences. Recognizing and building on positive experiences can foster a sense of achievement and motivation.

Skills, Questions, and Tasks:

- Life Exploration: Discuss future aspirations. Question: "What do you want to explore in your life?"
- Positive Experiences: Reflect on positive experiences. Task: Write about three positive experiences and how they made you feel.

Week 6: Stress Awareness & Stress Management

Introduction: We will focus on stress awareness and management techniques. Understanding the sources and signs of stress and learning effective coping strategies will help youth maintain emotional balance.

Skills, Questions, and Tasks:

- Stress Awareness: Identify sources of stress. Task: List familiar sources of stress in your life.
- Stress Management: Practice stress management techniques. Task: Try strategies such as deep breathing, exercise, or mindfulness and record their effects.

Week 7: Problem Solving

Introduction: We will explore problem-solving skills. Practical problem-solving abilities are essential for navigating challenges and making informed decisions.

Skills, Questions, and Tasks:

- Problem Solving: Develop a problem-solving plan. Task: Identify a current problem and create a step-by-step plan.
- Reflection: Reflect on past problem-solving successes. Question: "Can you describe when you successfully solved a problem?"

Week 8: Self-Care Tips, Positive Steps for Wellbeing, Healthy Choices, and Final Self-Care Assessment

Introduction: In the final week, we will review self-care tips, positive steps for well-being, and healthy choices. We will also conduct a final self-care assessment to evaluate progress and identify areas for continued growth.

Skills, Questions, and Tasks:

- Self-Care Tips: Learn self-care strategies. Task: Implement three new self-care activities.
- Positive Steps for Wellbeing: Plan steps for well-being. Task: Create a personal well-being plan.
- Healthy Choices: Discuss healthy lifestyle choices. Question: "What healthy choices can you make daily?"
- Final Self-Care Assessment: Conduct a final self-care assessment. Task: Complete the self-care evaluation and compare it to the initial assessment.

Overall Conclusion

This Empowerment Course is designed to provide parents, guardians, and trusted adults with the tools and knowledge to support youth in developing resilience and coping skills. By focusing on critical areas such as stress management, success, gratitude, self-esteem, protective factors, stages of change, social supports, values, strengths, and problem-solving, you will be well-equipped to guide youth through their challenges and help them thrive. Remember, your role is crucial in creating a supportive environment that fosters growth and empowerment. I appreciate your commitment to this vital journey.

Empowerment Course for Youth

Course Overview

Welcome to the Empowerment Course, designed to help you develop resilience and coping skills. This self-paced course will cover essential topics such as stress management, success, gratitude, self-esteem, protective factors, stages of change, social supports, values, strengths, and problem-solving. By the end of this course, you will have the tools to navigate challenges and thrive in your personal and academic life.

Course Objectives

By the end of this course, you will be able to:

1. Understand and apply the stages of change to your personal growth.
2. Identify protective factors and build strong social support.
3. Practice gratitude through exercises and journaling.
4. Build self-esteem by exploring your values, strengths, and positive qualities.
5. Use stress management techniques effectively.
6. Develop strong problem-solving skills.
7. Implement self-care and make healthy choices for overall well-being.

Age-Specific Empowerment Skills Stories

Child (Ages 5-10)

Story Overview: Emma, an 8-year-old girl, faced the challenge of adjusting to a new school after her family moved to a different city.

Experiences: Emma struggled with making new friends and feeling confident in her new environment. She often felt lonely and anxious.

Overcoming Barriers: With the support of her parents and teachers, Emma learned to manage her anxiety through breathing exercises and positive affirmations. She joined a school club, which helped her make friends and build confidence.

Role of Parents/Guardians and Trusted Adults: Emma's parents played a crucial role by encouraging her to express her feelings, providing reassurance, and fostering new social connections. Her teacher also supported her by creating a welcoming classroom environment.

Skills, Questions, and Tasks:

- Stress Management: Teach Emma breathing exercises. Question: "How do you feel after doing the breathing exercise?"
- Success: Celebrate small achievements. Task: Create a "Success Jar" where Emma can drop notes of her daily successes.
- Gratitude: Start a gratitude journal. Task: Write three things Emma is grateful for each day.
- Self-Esteem: Identify strengths. Question: "What do you like most about yourself?"

- Protective Factors: Encourage participation in group activities. Task: Join a club or team.
- Stages of Change: Discuss feelings about the new school. Question: "How do you feel about your new school now compared to when you first started?"
- Social Supports: Help her make friends. Task: Plan a playdate with a classmate.
- Values: Discuss what is important to her. Question: "What do you think is the most important quality in a friend?"
- Strengths: Identify and praise her strengths. Task: Draw a picture of herself doing something she's good at.
- Problem Solving: Role-play social scenarios. Task: Practice introducing herself and asking to join in games.

Adolescent (Ages 11-13)

Story Overview: Liam, a 12-year-old boy, struggled with bullying at school and found it challenging to cope with the stress and self-esteem issues that resulted from it.

Experiences: Liam felt isolated and scared to go to school. His grades began to slip, and he became withdrawn.

Overcoming Barriers: With the help of a school counselor, Liam learned strategies to deal with bullying, such as seeking help from trusted adults and practicing assertiveness. He also joined a martial arts class to build confidence and resilience.

Role of Parents/Guardians and Trusted Adults: Liam's parents and school counselor provided support by addressing the bullying issue with school authorities and encouraging Liam to talk about his experiences. The martial arts instructor also served as a positive role model.

Skills, Questions, and Tasks:

- Stress Management: Teach stress management techniques. Task: Practice deep breathing and relaxation exercises.
- Success: Set and achieve small goals. Question: "What is one thing you accomplished today that you are proud of?"
- Gratitude: Keep a gratitude journal. Task: Write three things Liam is grateful for each day.
- Self-Esteem: Encourage positive self-talk. Question: "What positive things can you say to yourself when you feel down?"
- Protective Factors: Identify supportive adults. Task: Make a list of trusted adults he can talk to.
- Stages of Change: Reflect on his feelings. Question: "How have your feelings about school changed since you started working on this?"
- Social Supports: Build a support network. Task: Identify friends and adults who can offer support.
- Values: Discuss his values. Question: "What qualities do you admire in others?"
- Strengths: Recognize and celebrate strengths. Task: List five personal strengths.
- Problem Solving: Develop a problem-solving plan. Task: Create a step-by-step plan to address a current problem.

Teen (Ages 14-18)

Story Overview: Sophia, a 16-year-old girl, faced the challenge of balancing academic pressures with her responsibilities at home, leading to high stress and burnout.

Experiences: Sophia felt overwhelmed by her schoolwork and family duties. She struggled with time management and experienced frequent stress.

Overcoming Barriers: Sophia learned stress management techniques such as time management, prioritizing tasks, and taking breaks. She also sought support from her teachers and joined a study group to manage her academic workload better.

Role of Parents/Guardians and Trusted Adults: Sophia's parents supported her by helping her set realistic goals and encouraging her to take breaks. Her teachers provided additional academic support and resources.

Skills, Questions, and Tasks:

- Stress Management: Teach effective stress management strategies. Task: Create a daily schedule that includes time for relaxation.
- Success: Celebrate academic achievements. Question: "What are you most proud of achieving this week?"
- Gratitude: Maintain a gratitude journal. Task: Write about three things Sophia is grateful for each day.
- Self-Esteem: Encourage self-reflection and positive affirmations. Question: "What positive qualities do you see in yourself?"
- Protective Factors: Identify supportive people and resources. Task: Make a list of supportive teachers and friends.

- Stages of Change: Discuss her progress. Question: "How has your approach to balancing responsibilities changed over time?"
- Social Supports: Strengthen her support network. Task: Identify people she can rely on for support and encouragement.
- Values: Reflect on her values. Question: "What are your core values, and how do they influence your decisions?"
- Strengths: Identify and utilize strengths. Task: List strengths and think about how they help in daily tasks.
- Problem Solving: Develop problem-solving skills. Task: Identify a current challenge and create a plan to address it.

Weekly Modules

Week 1: The Stages of Change and a Self-Care Assessment

Introduction: Welcome to Week 1! This week, we will learn about the stages of change and do a self-care assessment. Understanding the stages of change will help you recognize where you are in your growth journey. The self-care evaluation will help you see how well you care for yourself.

Content:

Stages of Change Model

The Stages of Change model, or the Transtheoretical Model, describes individuals' processes when changing behavior. It includes six stages:

1. Precontemplation (Not Ready)

- Characteristics: Individuals still need to consider change. They may be unaware of the need for change or in denial about the consequences of their behavior.
- Mindset: "I don't have a problem" or "I don't need to change."
- Strategies: Increase awareness of the problem, provide information, and encourage self-reflection.

2. Contemplation (Getting Ready)

- Characteristics: Individuals recognize the need for change and start to think about it. They weigh the pros and cons but have yet to commit to action.
- Mindset: "I might change" or "I'm thinking about it."
- Strategies: Discuss the benefits of change, address barriers, and encourage the exploration of options.

3. Preparation (Ready)

- Characteristics: Individuals intend to take action soon and may start making small changes. They develop a plan and gather resources.
- Mindset: "I will change" or "I'm planning to change."
- Strategies: Help create a detailed action plan, set realistic goals, and provide support and resources.

4. Action

- Characteristics: Individuals actively implement their plans and change their behavior significantly. This stage requires the most effort and commitment.
- Mindset: "I am changing" or "I'm doing it."
- Strategies: Provide encouragement, monitor progress, and offer problem-solving support.

5. Maintenance

- Characteristics: Individuals work to sustain the changes and prevent relapse. They integrate new behaviors into their lifestyle.
- Mindset: "I have changed" or "I'm maintaining it."
- Strategies: Reinforce positive behaviors, develop coping strategies for potential triggers, and celebrate successes.

6. Relapse

- Characteristics: Individuals may revert to old behaviors. Relapse is common and can be part of the learning process.
- Mindset: "I slipped up" or "I need to try again."
- Strategies: Analyze the reasons for relapse, learn from the experience, and re-enter the cycle at an appropriate stage.

Self-Care Assessment

A Self-Care Assessment helps individuals evaluate how well they meet their physical, emotional, social, and spiritual needs. Here's a breakdown of each area:

Physical Self-Care

- Components: Nutrition, exercise, sleep, medical care, and hygiene.
- Questions to Ask:
    - Am I eating a balanced diet?
    - Do I get regular physical activity?
    - Am I getting enough sleep?
    - Do I attend regular medical check-ups?
    - Do I maintain good personal hygiene?

Emotional Self-C care

- Components: Stress management, emotional expression, and mental health.
- Questions to Ask:
    - How do I manage stress?
    - Do I allow myself to express my emotions?
    - Am I aware of my emotional needs?
    - Do I seek help when needed (e.g., therapy, counseling)?

Social Self-Care

- Components: Relationships, social support, and community involvement.
- Questions to Ask:
    - Do I have supportive relationships?
    - Do I spend quality time with friends and family?
    - Am I involved in my community?

- Do I set boundaries in my relationships?

Spiritual Self-Care

- Components: Personal values, beliefs, and practices that provide meaning and purpose.
- Questions to Ask:
    - Do I engage in activities that align with my values and beliefs?
    - Do I take time for reflection and mindfulness?
    - Am I involved in spiritual or religious practices that fulfill me?
    - Do I feel a sense of purpose and meaning in my life?

Conducting a Self-Care Assessment

1. Reflect: Take time to think about each area of self-care and how well you are meeting your needs.
2. Rate: Use a scale (e.g., 1-10) to rate your satisfaction in each area.
3. Identify Gaps: Note any areas where you feel you need improvement.
4. Set Goals: Create specific, actionable goals to enhance self-care in the identified areas.
5. Monitor Progress: Regularly review and adjust your self-care practices to ensure they continue to meet your needs.

By understanding the Stages of Change and conducting a thorough Self-Care Assessment, you can better manage personal growth and well-being.

Activities:

- Learn about the different stages of change.

- Complete a self-care assessment to see where you can improve.

Skills, Questions, and Tasks:

- Question: "Can you think of a time you made a big change in your life?"
- Task: Reflect on your self-care assessment results and choose one area to work on.

Week 2: Protective Factors and Social Supports

Introduction: In Week 2, we will focus on identifying protective factors and building social support. These elements are crucial for staying strong and resilient when life gets tough.

Content:

Protective Factors

Protective factors are conditions or attributes that help individuals cope with stress and reduce the likelihood of adverse outcomes. They enhance resilience and promote well-being.

Types of Protective Factors

1. Individual Factors

- Self-esteem: A positive self-image and self-worth
- Problem-solving skills: Ability to tackle challenges effectively
- Emotional regulation: Managing emotions in a healthy way
- Optimism: Maintaining a positive outlook on life

2. Family Factors

- Supportive family relationships: Strong bonds with family members
- Clear expectations: Consistent rules and boundaries at home
- Family cohesion: A sense of unity and togetherness
- Open communication: Ability to discuss issues freely within the family

3. Community Factors

- Positive school environment: A supportive and engaging educational setting
- Extracurricular activities: Involvement in sports, arts, or other interests
- Safe neighborhoods: Living in an area with low crime rates and community resources
- Access to support services: Availability of mental health and social services

4. Cultural Factors

- Cultural solid identity: Connection to one's cultural heritage
- Cultural practices and beliefs: Traditions that provide meaning and support
- Community involvement: Participation in cultural events and activities

Benefits of Protective Factors

- Increase resilience to stress and adversity
- Promote positive mental health outcomes
- Enhance coping mechanisms
- Foster personal growth and development

Social Supports

Social supports refer to the network of people and resources an individual can rely on for emotional, practical, and informational assistance.

Types of Social Supports

1. Friends

- Peer support: Emotional understanding from those of similar age or experience
- Shared activities: Engaging in enjoyable activities together
- Mutual trust: Having confidants to share personal matters

2. Family

- Unconditional love: Acceptance and support regardless of circumstances
- Guidance: Advice and wisdom from older family members
- Practical support: Help with daily needs and challenges

3. Mentors

- Role models: Individuals who inspire and guide personal growth
- Professional guidance: Career or academic advice from experienced individuals
- Skill development: Learning from those with expertise in specific areas

4. Clubs and Organizations

- Shared interests: Connecting with others who have similar hobbies or goals
- Structured activities: Regular meetings or events that provide social interaction
- Leadership opportunities: Chances to develop skills and take on responsibilities

5. Online Communities

- Virtual support: Connecting with others facing similar challenges
- Information sharing: Access to resources and experiences from a diverse group
- Accessibility: Support is available regardless of geographic location

Benefits of Social Supports

- Reduce feelings of isolation and loneliness
- Provide emotional comfort during difficult times
- Offer practical assistance with daily challenges
- Enhance self-esteem and sense of belonging
- Promote healthy behaviors through positive influence

Developing and Maintaining Social Supports

1. Cultivate existing relationships: Strengthen bonds with current friends and family
2. Join groups or clubs: Seek out organizations aligned with your interests
3. Volunteer: Engage in community service to meet like-minded individuals
4. Attend community events: Participate in local activities to expand your network
5. Seek professional connections: Find mentors or join professional associations

6. Use social media mindfully: Connect with others online while maintaining healthy boundaries
7. Be reciprocal: Offer support to others to build mutually beneficial relationships

Individuals can build a strong foundation for mental health, resilience, and overall well-being by understanding and actively developing protective factors and social supports.

Activities:

- Identify the protective factors in your life.
- Map out your social support network.

Skills, Questions, and Tasks:

- Question: "Who can you turn to for support?"
- Task: List five protective factors in your life and how they help you.

Week 3: Love Languages, Gratitude Exercises, Gratitude Journal & Thank You Letter

Introduction: Welcome to Week 3! This week, we will learn about love languages and practice gratitude. Understanding how you give and receive love can improve your relationships. Practicing gratitude can make you happier and more positive.

Content:

- Love Languages: Words of affirmation, acts of service, receiving gifts, quality time, and physical touch.

- Gratitude Practices: Write in a journal, exercise gratitude, and thank you letters.

Activities:

- Take a quiz to learn your language of love.
- Start a gratitude journal and write down things you are thankful for daily.
- Write a thank you letter to someone who has helped you.

Skills, Questions, and Tasks:

- Question: "How do you feel when practicing gratitude daily?"
- Task: Identify your love language and consider how to use it to improve your relationships with others.

Week 4: Values Exploration, My Strengths/Qualities & Self-Esteem

Introduction: In Week 4, we will explore your values, identify your strengths and qualities, and work on building self-esteem. Knowing what you value and recognizing your strengths will help you feel more confident and optimistic about yourself.

Content:

Values Exploration

Understanding your values is crucial for making decisions that align with your core beliefs and lead to a fulfilling life.

Process of Values Exploration

1. Self-reflection: Take time to think about what truly matters to you.
2. Identify core values: Consider areas such as family, career, personal growth, community, etc.
3. Prioritize values: Rank your values in order of importance.
4. Examine conflicts: Recognize when values may conflict and how to resolve these conflicts.
5. Align actions with values: Make decisions and set goals that reflect your core values.

Common Personal Values

- Honesty
- Integrity
- Family
- Freedom
- Creativity
- Achievement
- Compassion
- Adventure
- Security
- Personal growth

Benefits of Values Exploration

- Clearer decision-making
- Increased sense of purpose
- Better alignment between actions and beliefs
- Enhanced personal satisfaction

Strengths/Qualities

Identifying your strengths and qualities helps you leverage your natural talents and build confidence.

Methods for Identifying Strengths

1. Self-assessment: Reflect on activities you excel at and enjoy.
2. Feedback from others: Ask friends, family, or colleagues about your perceived strengths.
3. Personality assessments: Take tests like StrengthsFinder or Myers-Briggs Type Indicator.
4. Past successes: Analyze your achievements to identify underlying strengths.
5. Challenges overcome: Consider difficulties you've successfully navigated.

Categories of Strengths

- Cognitive: Problem-solving, critical thinking, creativity
- Interpersonal: Communication, empathy, leadership
- Intrapersonal: Self-awareness, resilience, adaptability
- Technical: Specific skills or knowledge in particular areas

Applying Strengths

- Focus on roles and tasks that utilize your strengths
- Develop complementary skills to enhance your natural talents
- Use strengths to overcome challenges in weaker areas

Self-Esteem

Building a positive self-image is essential for mental health, confidence, and well-being.

Components of Self-Esteem

1. Self-worth: Believing in your inherent value as a person

2. Self-efficacy: Confidence in your abilities to handle life's challenges
3. Self-respect: Treating yourself with kindness and respect

Strategies for Building Self-Esteem

1. Positive self-talk: Replace negative thoughts with positive, realistic ones
2. Set achievable goals: Accomplish small tasks to build confidence
3. Practice self-compassion: Treat yourself with the same kindness you'd offer a friend
4. Challenge negative beliefs: Question and reframe self-limiting thoughts
5. Celebrate successes: Acknowledge and appreciate your achievements, big and small
6. Engage in self-care: Prioritize physical and mental health
7. Surround yourself with positivity: Spend time with supportive people
8. Learn new skills: Expand your abilities to boost confidence
9. Help others: Volunteering or assisting others can increase self-worth
10. Accept compliments: Internalize positive feedback from others

Signs of Healthy Self-Esteem

- Confidence in your abilities
- Ability to say "no" when appropriate
- Willingness to try new things
- Resilience in the face of setbacks
- Assertiveness in expressing needs and opinions

Benefits of High Self-Esteem

- Improved relationships
- Better mental health
- Increased resilience to stress
- Greater life satisfaction
- Enhanced performance in work and personal life

By exploring your values, identifying your strengths, and building self-esteem, you create a strong foundation for personal growth and fulfillment. These elements help you make authentic choices, leverage your natural talents, and approach life with confidence and positivity.

Activities:

- Reflect on your values and write them down.
- List your strengths and qualities.
- Practice self-esteem exercises.

Skills, Questions, and Tasks:

- Question: "What values guide your decisions and actions?"
- Task: List your strengths and qualities and consider how to use them daily.

Week 5: Life Exploration and Positive Experiences

Introduction: Welcome to Week 5! This week, we will explore different aspects of your life and reflect on positive experiences. Recognizing and building on positive experiences can help you feel more accomplished and motivated.

Content:

Life Exploration

Life exploration involves examining your interests, hobbies, and future goals to understand better yourself and what you want.

1. Interests

Process of Exploring Interests:

- Reflect on activities you enjoy
- Try new experiences
- Pay attention to what captures your attention
- Consider subjects you would like to learn about

Types of Interests:

- Academic (e.g., science, literature, history)
- Creative (e.g., art, music, writing)
- Physical (e.g., sports, dance, outdoor activities)
- Social (e.g., community service, leadership roles)
- Technological (e.g., coding, robotics, digital media)

2. Hobbies

Benefits of Hobbies:

- Stress relief
- Skill development
- Social Connections
- Personal fulfillment

Exploring Hobbies:

- Try different activities
- Join clubs or groups
- Take classes or workshops
- Watch tutorials or read about potential hobbies

3. Future Goals

Types of Goals:

- Career goals
- Educational goals
- Personal development goals
- Relationship goals
- Financial goals

Goal-Setting Process:

1. Identify areas of importance in your life
2. Envision your ideal future
3. Set SMART goals (Specific, Measurable, Achievable, Relevant, Time-bound)
4. Break long-term goals into short-term objectives
5. Create action plans to achieve your goals

Benefits of Life Exploration:

- Increased self-awareness
- Better decision-making for future choices
- Enhanced motivation and purpose
- Improved life satisfaction

Positive Experiences

Reflecting on positive experiences involves consciously recalling and appreciating good things that have happened to you.

Importance of Reflecting on Positive Experiences:

- Boosts mood and overall well-being
- Increases gratitude and optimism
- Builds resilience for facing challenges
- Enhances self-esteem and confidence

Types of Positive Experiences to Reflect On:

1. Personal Achievements
    - Academic or professional successes
    - Overcoming personal challenges
    - Learning new skills
2. Relationships
    - Meaningful connections with friends and family
    - Acts of kindness received from others
    - Positive interactions or collaborations
3. Moments of Joy
    - Fun outings or vacations
    - Celebrations and special occasions
    - Simple pleasures in everyday life
4. Growth Experiences
    - Lessons learned from difficulties
    - Moments of personal insight

- Times when you stepped out of your comfort zone
5. Acts of Kindness
    - Times when you helped others
    - Volunteering experiences
    - The positive impact you've had on others

Techniques for Reflecting on Positive Experiences:

1. Gratitude Journaling
    - Write down three good things that happen each day
    - Describe why these experiences were meaningful
2. Positive Visualization
    - Take time to recall positive memories vividly
    - Engage all senses in remembering the experience
3. Sharing with Others
    - Discuss positive experiences with friends or family
    - Express appreciation to those involved in your positive experiences
4. Creating a "Happiness Jar"
    - Write down positive experiences on slips of paper
    - Collect them in a jar to review later
5. Photo Reflection
    - Look through photos of happy moments
    - Recall the emotions and details of those experiences
6. Mindful Appreciation
    - Practice being present and noticing positive aspects of current experiences

Benefits of Reflecting on Positive Experiences:

- Improved emotional regulation
- Increased life satisfaction
- Enhanced ability to cope with stress
- Stronger, more positive relationships
- Greater appreciation for life's moments

By exploring life and regularly reflecting on positive experiences, you can gain a clearer sense of direction, increase your overall happiness, and build a more fulfilling life. These practices contribute to personal growth, emotional well-being, and a more optimistic outlook.

Activities:

- Explore different areas of your life and think about what you enjoy.
- Reflect on three positive experiences and how they made you feel.

Skills, Questions, and Tasks:

- Question: "What are some activities or hobbies you enjoy?"
- Task: Write about three positive experiences and why they were meaningful.

Week 6: Stress Awareness & Stress Management

Introduction: In Week 6, we will learn about stress awareness and management techniques. Understanding what causes stress and how to manage it will help you stay calm and focused.

Content:

Deep Breathing Techniques

1. Diaphragmatic Breathing:
   - Breathe deeply from your diaphragm
   - Inhale through your nose, exhale through your mouth
   - Practice for 5-10 minutes daily
2. 4-7-8 Breathing:
   - Inhale for four counts
   - Hold your breath for seven counts
   - Exhale for eight counts
   - Repeat four times

Exercise

1. Aerobic Exercise:
   - Jogging, swimming, cycling
   - Aim for 30 minutes, 3-5 times a week
2. Strength Training:
   - Weight lifting, bodyweight exercises
   - 2-3 sessions per week
3. Yoga:
   - Combines physical postures, breathing techniques, and meditation
   - Practice 2-3 times a week

Mindfulness Techniques

1. Meditation:
   - Focus on breathing or a mantra
   - Start with 5-10 minutes daily
   - Gradually increase duration
2. Body Scan:

- Systematically focus attention on different parts of your body
- Notice sensations without judgment
3. Mindful Walking:
    - Pay attention to each step and your surroundings
    - Practice outdoors or indoors

Additional Stress Management Techniques

1. Time Management:
    - Prioritize tasks
    - Break large projects into smaller steps
    - Use calendars and to-do lists
2. Progressive Muscle Relaxation:
    - Tense and relax different muscle groups
    - Practice before bed or during breaks
3. Journaling:
    - Write about stressors and emotions
    - Identify patterns and potential solutions
4. Social Support:
    - Connect with friends and family
    - Join support groups or seek professional help if needed
5. Healthy Lifestyle Habits:
    - Maintain a balanced diet
    - Get adequate sleep (7-9 hours per night)
    - Limit caffeine and alcohol intake
6. Hobbies and Leisure Activities:
    - Engage in activities you enjoy
    - Make time for relaxation and fun
7. Cognitive Restructuring:
    - Challenge negative thoughts
    - Reframe situations in a more positive or realistic light

Implementing Stress Management

1. Assess Your Current Stress Levels:
   - Use stress scales or questionnaires
   - Keep a stress diary
2. Identify Effective Techniques:
   - Try different methods
   - Note which ones work best for you
3. Create a Stress Management Plan:
   - Incorporate various techniques
   - Set realistic goals for practice
4. Practice Regularly:
   - Make stress management a daily habit
   - Be consistent in your approach
5. Monitor Progress:
   - Reassess stress levels periodically
   - Adjust techniques as needed
6. Seek Professional Help if Needed:
   - Consult a therapist or counselor for persistent stress

By developing stress awareness and implementing effective stress management techniques, you can significantly improve your ability to cope with life's challenges, enhance your overall well-being, and maintain better physical and mental health.

Activities:

- Identify familiar sources of stress in your life.
- Practice different stress management techniques.

Skills, Questions, and Tasks:

- Question: "What are some things that make you feel stressed?"

- Task: Try different stress management techniques and write the best for you.

Week 7: Problem Solving

Introduction: Welcome to Week 7! This week, we will focus on developing problem-solving skills. Solving problems effectively is an essential skill that will help you in many areas of your life.

Content:

Problem-Solving: A Step-by-Step Approach

1. Identify the Problem

Steps:

- Recognize the issue: Clearly define what the problem is.
- Be specific: Ensure the problem is stated in clear, concise terms.
- Gather information: Collect relevant data and facts to understand the problem entirely.

Example:

- Problem: "Our team is consistently missing project deadlines."

2. Analyze the Problem

Steps:

- Break down the problem: Divide the problem into smaller, manageable parts.

- Identify root causes: Use techniques like the 5 Whys or Fishbone Diagram to find underlying causes.
- Consider different perspectives: Look at the problem from various angles for a comprehensive view.

Example:

- Root causes: "Lack of clear communication, unrealistic deadlines, insufficient resources."

3. Generate Possible Solutions

Steps:

- Brainstorm ideas: Encourage creative thinking and list all potential solutions.
- Involve others: Get input from team members or stakeholders.
- Avoid judgment: During brainstorming, focus on quantity over quality; evaluate later.

Example:

- Possible solutions: "Improve communication channels, adjust project timelines, allocate more resources."

4. Evaluate and Select the Best Solution

Steps:

- Assess feasibility: Consider the practicality of each solution.
- Weigh pros and cons: Analyze the advantages and disadvantages of each option.

- Prioritize solutions: Rank solutions based on criteria such as effectiveness, cost, and time.

Example:

- Best solution: "Improve communication channels and adjust project timelines."

5. Develop an Action Plan

Steps:

- Outline steps: Create a detailed action plan for implementing the chosen solution.
- Assign responsibilities: Designate tasks to specific individuals or teams.
- Set deadlines: Establish clear timelines for each step of the plan.

Example:

- Action plan: "Implement weekly team meetings, use project management software, revise project schedules."

6. Implement the Solution

Steps:

- Execute the plan: Put the action plan into motion.
- Monitor progress: Track the implementation process and ensure tasks are being completed.
- Communicate: Keep all stakeholders informed about progress and any adjustments needed.

Example:

- Implementation: "Start weekly meetings, train the team on new software, and adjust project timelines."

7. Evaluate the Results

Steps:

- Review outcomes: Assess the effectiveness of the solution.
- Measure success: Use metrics and feedback to determine if the problem has been resolved.
- Identify lessons learned: Reflect on what worked well and what could be improved.

Example:

- Evaluation: "Project deadlines are now being met consistently, and team communication has improved."

8. Adjust and Improve

Steps:

- Make necessary adjustments: If the solution is ineffective, tweak the action plan.
- Continuous improvement: Use insights gained to improve future problem-solving efforts.
- Document the process: Keep records of the problem-solving process for future reference.

Example:

- Adjustments: "Further refine communication strategies, provide additional training on project management tools."

Benefits of a Step-by-Step Problem-Solving Approach

- Clarity: Provides a clear framework for addressing issues.
- Efficiency: Saves time by systematically tackling problems.
- Effectiveness: Increases the likelihood of finding successful solutions.
- Collaboration: Encourages teamwork and diverse input.
- Continuous Improvement: Facilitates learning and growth from each problem-solving experience.

This structured approach can enhance your problem-solving skills, leading to more effective and sustainable solutions to your challenges.

Activities:

- Identify a current problem you are facing.
- Create a step-by-step plan to solve the problem.

Skills, Questions, and Tasks:

- Question: "Can you describe when you successfully solved a problem?"
- Task: Work through a current problem using a step-by-step approach.

Week 8: Self-Care Tips, Positive Steps for Wellbeing, Healthy Choices, and Final Self-Care Assessment

Introduction: In the final week, we will review self-care tips, positive steps for well-being, and healthy choices. We will also conduct a final self-care assessment to evaluate your progress and identify areas for continued growth.

Content:

Problem-Solving: A Step-by-Step Approach

1. Identify the Problem

Steps:

- Recognize the issue: Clearly define what the problem is.
- Be specific: Ensure the problem is stated in clear, concise terms.
- Gather information: Collect relevant data and facts to understand the problem entirely.

Example:

- Problem: "Our team is consistently missing project deadlines."

2. Analyze the Problem

Steps:

- Break down the problem: Divide the problem into smaller, manageable parts.
- Identify root causes: Use techniques like the 5 Whys or Fishbone Diagram to find underlying causes.

- Consider different perspectives: Look at the problem from various angles for a comprehensive view.

Example:

- Root causes: "Lack of clear communication, unrealistic deadlines, insufficient resources."

3. Generate Possible Solutions

Steps:

- Brainstorm ideas: Encourage creative thinking and list all potential solutions.
- Involve others: Get input from team members or stakeholders.
- Avoid judgment: During brainstorming, focus on quantity over quality; evaluate later.

Example:

- Possible solutions: "Improve communication channels, adjust project timelines, allocate more resources."

4. Evaluate and Select the Best Solution

Steps:

- Assess feasibility: Consider the practicality of each solution.
- Weigh pros and cons: Analyze the advantages and disadvantages of each option.
- Prioritize solutions: Rank solutions based on criteria such as effectiveness, cost, and time.

Example:

- Best solution: "Improve communication channels and adjust project timelines."

5. Develop an Action Plan

Steps:

- Outline steps: Create a detailed action plan for implementing the chosen solution.
- Assign responsibilities: Designate tasks to specific individuals or teams.
- Set deadlines: Establish clear timelines for each step of the plan.

Example:

- Action plan: "Implement weekly team meetings, use project management software, revise project schedules."

6. Implement the Solution

Steps:

- Execute the plan: Put the action plan into motion.
- Monitor progress: Track the implementation process and ensure tasks are being completed.
- Communicate: Keep all stakeholders informed about progress and any adjustments needed.

Example:

- Implementation: "Start weekly meetings, train the team on new software, and adjust project timelines."

7. Evaluate the Results

Steps:

- Review outcomes: Assess the effectiveness of the solution.
- Measure success: Use metrics and feedback to determine if the problem has been resolved.
- Identify lessons learned: Reflect on what worked well and what could be improved.

Example:

- Evaluation: "Project deadlines are now being met consistently, and team communication has improved."

8. Adjust and Improve

Steps:

- Make necessary adjustments: If the solution is ineffective, tweak the action plan.
- Continuous improvement: Use insights gained to improve future problem-solving efforts.
- Document the process: Keep records of the problem-solving process for future reference.

Example:

- Adjustments: "Further refine communication strategies, provide additional training on project management tools."

Benefits of a Step-by-Step Problem-Solving Approach

- Clarity: Provides a clear framework for addressing issues.
- Efficiency: Saves time by systematically tackling problems.
- Effectiveness: Increases the likelihood of finding successful solutions.
- Collaboration: Encourages teamwork and diverse input.
- Continuous Improvement: Facilitates learning and growth from each problem-solving experience.

This structured approach can enhance your problem-solving skills, leading to more effective and sustainable solutions to your challenges.

Self-Care Tips

Learning new self-care strategies can help you maintain and improve your physical, emotional, and mental health.

Physical Self-Care Tips

- Exercise regularly: Aim for at least 30 minutes of moderate exercise most days of the week.
- Eat a balanced diet: Include a variety of fruits, vegetables, lean proteins, and whole grains.
- Get enough sleep: Aim for 7-9 hours of quality sleep per night.
- Stay hydrated: Drink plenty of water throughout the day.
- Practice good hygiene: Maintain regular personal hygiene routines.

Emotional Self-Care Tips

- Practice mindfulness: Engage in mindfulness or meditation exercises to stay present.
- Express emotions: Find healthy ways to express your feelings, such as journaling or talking to a friend.
- Set boundaries: Learn to say no and set limits to protect your emotional well-being.
- Engage in hobbies: Spend time doing activities you enjoy that relax you.
- Seek professional help: Don't hesitate to contact a therapist or counselor if needed.

Social Self-Care Tips

- Maintain relationships: Stay connected with friends and family.
- Join groups: Participate in clubs, organizations, or community activities.
- Volunteer: Give back to your community through volunteer work.
- Communicate openly: Practice open and honest communication with those around you.
- Seek support: Be bold and ask for help when needed.

Spiritual Self-Care Tips

- Reflect: Spend time in reflection or meditation.
- Practice gratitude: Keep a gratitude journal to focus on positive aspects of life.
- Engage in spiritual practices: Participate in religious or spiritual activities that are meaningful to you.
- Connect with nature: Spend time outdoors to feel connected to the world around you.
- Find purpose: Engage in activities that give your life meaning and purpose.

Positive Steps for Wellbeing

Creating a personal well-being plan involves setting goals and strategies to enhance your health and happiness.

Steps to Create a Well-Being Plan

1. Assess Your Current Well-Being
   - Reflect on your physical, emotional, social, and spiritual health.
   - Identify areas where you feel strong and areas needing improvement.
2. Set Specific Goals
   - Define clear, achievable goals for each area of well-being.
   - Use the SMART criteria (Specific, Measurable, Achievable, Relevant, Time-bound).
3. Develop Action Steps
   - Outline specific actions you will take to achieve your goals.
   - Break down larger goals into smaller, manageable tasks.
4. Create a Schedule
   - Plan when and how often you will engage in your well-being activities.
   - Incorporate these activities into your daily or weekly routine.
5. Monitor Progress
   - Keep track of your progress toward your goals.
   - Adjust your plan as needed based on what is working and what isn't.
6. Seek Support
   - Share your plan with friends, family, or a mentor for accountability.
   - Join groups or communities that support your well-being goals.

Example of a Well-Being Plan

- Physical Goal: Exercise 4 times a week.
    - Action Steps: Join a gym, schedule workouts, and track progress.
- Emotional Goal: Practice mindfulness daily.
    - Action Steps: Download a meditation app, set a daily reminder, and write a journal about your experiences.
- Social Goal: Connect with friends weekly.
    - Action Steps: Schedule weekly meetups, join a club, and call a friend.
- Spiritual Goal: Reflect on gratitude daily.
    - Action Steps: Keep a gratitude journal; write three things you're grateful for daily.

Healthy Choices

Making choices that promote health and well-being involves adopting habits that support your physical, emotional, and mental health.

Examples of Healthy Choices

1. Nutrition
    - Choose whole, unprocessed foods.
    - Limit sugar, salt, and unhealthy fats.
    - Eat regular, balanced meals.
2. Physical Activity
    - Incorporate regular exercise into your routine.
    - Find activities you enjoy, such as walking, swimming, or dancing.
    - Stay active throughout the day, even with slight movements.
3. Mental Health

- Practice stress management techniques, such as deep breathing or yoga.
- Engage in activities that stimulate your mind, like reading or puzzles.
- Seek help if you're feeling overwhelmed or anxious.

4. Sleep
   - Establish a regular sleep schedule.
   - Create a relaxing bedtime routine.
   - Ensure your sleep environment is comfortable and free of distractions.
5. Substance Use
   - Limit alcohol consumption.
   - Avoid smoking and recreational drugs.
   - Use medications as prescribed by a healthcare professional.
6. Social Connections
   - Build and maintain strong relationships.
   - Participate in social activities.
   - Communicate openly and honestly with others.

Final Self-Care Assessment

Evaluating your self-care practices helps you understand what is working well and where you might need to make changes.

Steps for a Self-Care Assessment

1. Reflect on Each Area of Self-Care
   - Physical, emotional, social, and spiritual.
2. Rate Your Satisfaction
   - Use a scale (e.g., 1-10) to rate how well you meet your needs in each area.
3. Identify Strengths and Weaknesses
   - Note areas where you feel strong and areas needing improvement.

4. Set New Goals
    - Based on your assessment, set new self-care goals.
    - Use the SMART criteria to make these goals specific and achievable.
5. Create an Action Plan
    - Develop a plan to address areas needing improvement.
    - Include specific steps and a timeline for achieving your goals.
6. Monitor and Adjust
    - Regularly review your self-care practices.
    - Adjust your plan as needed to ensure it continues to meet your needs.

Example of a Self-Care Assessment

- Physical Self-Care: 7/10
    - Strengths: Regular exercise, balanced diet.
    - Weaknesses: Inconsistent sleep schedule.
    - New Goal: Establish a consistent bedtime routine.
- Emotional Self-Care: 6/10
    - Strengths: Journaling, mindfulness practice.
    - Weaknesses: Difficulty managing stress.
    - New Goal: Practice deep breathing exercises daily.
- Social Self-Care: 8/10
    - Strengths: Strong relationships and regular social activities.
    - Weaknesses: Need to set better boundaries.
    - New Goal: Learn to say no and set limits.
- Spiritual Self-Care: 5/10
    - Strengths: Occasional reflection and gratitude practice.
    - Weaknesses: Lack of regular spiritual activities.

- New Goal: Spend 10 minutes daily in reflection or meditation.

You can enhance your overall health and well-being by learning new self-care strategies, creating a personal well-being plan, making healthy choices, and regularly assessing your self-care practices. These steps help you maintain balance, reduce stress, and lead a more fulfilling life.

Activities:

- Implement three new self-care activities.
- Create a personal well-being plan.
- Complete the final self-care assessment and compare it to your initial assessment.

Skills, Questions, and Tasks:

- Question: "What healthy choices can you make daily?"
- Task: Write a well-being plan and list three new self-care activities to try.

Overall Conclusion

This Empowerment Course is designed to provide you with the tools and knowledge to build resilience and coping skills. By focusing on stress management, success, gratitude, self-esteem, protective factors, stages of change, social supports, values, strengths, and problem-solving, you will be well-equipped to face challenges and thrive. Remember, your journey is unique, and with the right strategies and support, you can achieve your goals and maintain your well-being. Thank you for participating in this important journey of self-discovery and growth.

Key Note:

Any references to historical events, real people, or real places are used fictitiously. Names, characters, and places are products of the author's imagination.

www.youthsuccesscoaching.org

www.ingramcontent.com/pod-product-compliance
Lightning Source LLC
Chambersburg PA
CBHW052030030426
42337CB00027B/4943